INSECTS

INSECTS

AN EDIBLE
FIELD GUIDE

STEFAN GATES

EBURY
PRESS

1 3 5 7 9 10 8 6 4 2

Ebury Press, an imprint of Ebury Publishing,
20 Vauxhall Bridge Road,
London, SW1V 2SA

Ebury Press is part of the Penguin Random House group of companies
whose addresses can be found at global.penguinrandomhouse.com

Copyright © Stefan Gates 2017
Illustrations © Candela Riveros 2017

Angela Hartnett has asserted her right to be identified as the author of this
Work in accordance with the Copyright, Designs and Patents Act 1988

First published by Ebury Press in 2017

www.penguin.co.uk

A CIP catalogue record for this book is available from the British Library

Design: seagulls.net
Cover Design: Grade Design

ISBN: 978-1-785-03525-8

Printed and bound by Clays Ltd, St Ives plc

Penguin Random House is committed to a sustainable future for
our business, our readers and our planet. This book is made from
Forest Stewardship Council® certified paper.

MIX
Paper from
responsible sources
FSC® C018179
www.fsc.org

To Stanley.

CONTENTS

INTRODUCTION

Hail, adventurer!

I am delighted that you've opened this humble little book and taken the first step on your entomophagic adventure, but I am also aware that you may be harbouring a violent subconscious revulsion to our six-legged friends. It will come as no surprise that a toddler in northern Thailand squeals with delight when presented with a bowl of freshly cooked crickets while most of us grow up thinking that insects are dirty, otherworldly creepy crawlies put on this earth largely to scare the bejesus out of us. It would be obtuse of me to dismiss these feelings, not least because even I must confess to a vestigial distaste very occasionally rising to the surface when faced with a gruesome new invertebrate staring back at me.

As with so many life-affirming adventures, however, the path to wisdom may be challenging, but the rewards commensurately uplifting. So consider your hand held firmly within my grasp and let us skip together towards gastronomic enlightenment with joy in our hearts and a Colombian fat-arsed ant in our teeth!

When I first caught the entomophagy bug, the one thing I lacked was a simple, clear field guide that would bring together all the fragments of information (of wildly varying quality) that are currently available. There are a handful of excellent publications around, especially from the admirably forward-thinking UN Food and Agriculture Organisation, but the subject is underrepresented in current literature, probably because of Western distaste. I hope that the book you hold in your hands will close this gap and lead to your own adventure.

MY TOP 10
EDIBLE INSECT DISHES

Although insect-eating is still in its early stages in Europe, a plethora of insect-based dishes can be found around the globe. Check off the ones you've tried here (and add ones you find as you explore):

- ❏ *1. Red ant salad.*

- ❏ *2. Chappulines.*

- ❏ *3. Colombian fat-arsed ants.*

- ❏ *4. Crickets with smoked herbs and stock.*

- ❏ *5. Palm weevils.*

- ❏ *6. Bamboo grubs.*

- ❏ *7. Freshly fried Cambodian grasshoppers.*

- ❏ *8. Thai primary school lunch: crickets fried with pandan leaves.*

- ❏ *9. Earthworm stir-fry.*

- ❏ *10. London woodlouse salad.*

LET'S START OFF ON THE RIGHT FOOT: WHAT IS AN INSECT?

The word 'insect' comes from the Latin for 'cut into sections'. There are over 1 million described species of insect (with estimates of the actual total ranging from 2.6-10 million), and they have specific defining features. They are invertebrates (i.e. lacking a backbone) made up of three main body sections: head, thorax and abdomen. They have a chitinous exoskeleton (chitinous material is made of a long-chain polymer derivative of glucose, and an exoskeleton is an exterior casing that holds the insect together). Other common elements are three pairs of jointed legs, two antennae and compound eyes. They have one of two life cycles: complete metamorphosis where the egg hatches into a larvae then pupates into its adult form, or incomplete metamorphosis where the nymph shows little difference from adults. Some will produce wings in the final moult (also known as the final instar) if adults are winged, and there are estimated to be 10 quintillion of them on earth (that's 10,000,000,000,000,000,000).

The thing is, we need to eat more insects. Lots more. And to ease their passage through your alimentary canal, perhaps we should begin by basking in the glow of some heartwarming facts:

* Insects taste delicious. I will prove it. (see p.11)

* Two billion people across the world eat insects on a regular basis. (see p.12)

* You're already eating insects, even if you don't know it. (see p.13)

* Culinary adventure is both invigorating and necessary. We shall take the potato as a case in point. (see p.14)

* Entomophagy could help save the planet. (see pp.21–22)

* Insects are highly nutritious. (see p.23)

* They really do taste delicious.

TASTE

The most common misconception about entomophagy (promulgated by certain popular jungle challenge TV shows) is that insects are a gruesome food, eaten raw, live and wriggly. The reality is very different. Very few insects are eaten raw because cooks across the world are clever and they care about both hygiene and flavour. Cooking them kills most bacteria that they may carry, and it also tends to destroy the efficacy of any toxins that they might contain.

But it gets more exciting when we look at their flavour profile: insects have a fascinating anatomy that lends itself to complex flavour chemistry for two reasons: firstly they are very high in protein (13-77% dry matter depending on insect order and life-stage, which makes mealworms and other caterpillars largely comparable to beef), with an excellent amino acid profile. Secondly they have a high surface area-to-volume ratio. These two elements allow splendorous Maillard reactions to take place on a huge scale. These are chemical reactions (specifically a cascading series of non-enzymatic browning reactions between amino acids and reducing sugars that thrive between 140-165C) that every cook craves because it leads to the classic fulsomeness of well-browned foods: the beefiness of seared steaks, the drool-inducing, umami-drenched triumph of a rotisserie-roasted chicken and the sheer toastiness of toast – all of these flavour profiles are the result of Maillard reactions. And the same goes for insects, so a handful of deep-fried grasshoppers will often smell and taste surprisingly beefy, but with a uniquely crunchy texture.

I've given tasting notes for the insects in this book at my peril because flavour profiles are variable and inconsistent. Much as a beautifully barbecued chicken wing will taste wildly different to a tarragon-poached chicken supreme (God forbid), I've eaten freshly fried waterbugs that smacked of pistachio, but others that were musty, like rising damp.

Like any food, insects can taste fantastic or bloody awful depending on a number of factors, mainly to do with chemistry, freshness, culinary skill and the quality of the ingredients they are cooked with. And a little local knowledge goes a long way, too.

My first mouthful of mopane worms was the very quintessence of dust (no one had told me that mopane worms are supposed to be rehydrated before eating) and if you are inquisitive enough to buy a pack of freeze-dried European-produced insects, do bear in mind that they will, much like a dried lentil, taste infinitely better when soaked in a little fragrant stock before use. Imagine freeze-drying a piece of beef fillet and then trying to enjoy it. Nobody's a winner there. The freeze-drying process is very useful as it ensures that no pathogens will be carried by the food, and they will receive the gift of a long shelf-life. But rehydrate that baby and add some good fat, and it'll repay you in spades.

By-and-large, the majority of pre-cooked insects bought at markets and roadside stalls are deep-fried. Nutritionally this isn't great, I grant you, but for simplicity, hygiene and flavour it's wonderful. There are a few insects that *are* eaten raw, of course: witchetty grubs are sometimes eaten fresh and wriggly, and, one of my favourites, red ants, are eaten raw but not alive, but these are rare exceptions.

TWO BILLION PEOPLE ACROSS THE WORLD EAT INSECTS

So you're in great company.

It's rare to find a culture where insects are the absolute main protein source, but the UN's Food and Agriculture Organisation estimates that around two billion people regularly supplement their diet with entomophagy, sometimes as a snack and sometimes as an important nutritional top-up, but never (in my experience) as an unwelcome necessity inflicted by poverty. On the contrary, insects are most likely to be bought at a premium, are more expensive than most other meats, and are consumed either as a treat or offered to guests as a great honour.

Over 1,900 insect species have been recorded as used for food across the world, with beetles, caterpillars and Hymenoptera (bees, wasps and ants) leading the charge. This book covers just over 70, mainly because in culinary terms there are many overlapping species, so it made sense to concentrate on those you are most likely to stumble across. I should also confess to the handful of entries that aren't (to entomologists' annoyance, I suspect) actually insects at all, such as spiders (arachnids, not insects), worms (phylum *Annelida*, not insects) and woodlice (isopod crustaceans). These have been included regardless, as they fall under the umberella of creatures most people think of as 'creepy-crawlies' (and they're damn tasty).

YOU'RE ALREADY EATING INSECTS, EVEN IF YOU DON'T KNOW IT.

The next time you eat supermarket-bought sausages, pink gummy sweets, pink sherbets, marshmallows or, frankly, any pink food whatsoever, take a good look at the label. If it says 'cochineal', 'E120' or 'carmines', you are eating powdered and processed cochineal bugs. They make a beautifully rich dye and the food manufacturer can use the phrase 'No Artificial Colours' on the label. Campari's rich red colour was derived from cochineal at least until 2006 and the dye is currently widely used for its depth of colour and excellent stability. Basically, if you're living in the West it's impossible to avoid eating cochineal once in a while.

If you're eating crushed scale insects already, why not multiple-regurgitated insect vomit? Or as it's more politely known: honey. Now we're on a roll. Then there's the sheer volume of insects and insect fragments that inevitably find their way into any food grown outside; not just salads, vegetables, tea and herbs but also cereals and the vast range of foods made from cereals: pasta, bread, cakes, pastries (see p.111).

CULINARY ADVENTURE: PRETENTIOUS NEOPHILIA?

Excellent question. Let us consider the potato.

The potato first arrived in Europe some years after Colombus discovered the Americas (which was some years after the Vikings had discovered them, and some more years again after the inhabitants had presumably discovered them themselves but let's not get bogged down in a post-colonial slanging match). It was introduced to the Old World by the Spanish in the late 16th century, and was initially thought of as a rather creepy novelty food (much as insects are now) alongside other important foods such as chillies, corn and tomatoes. Many of these imported foods were grown by the aristocracy both as botanical curios and as displays of wealth, especially during the Restoration period and later. On one level it was sheer aristocratic one-upmanship but it also launched staple crops that sustained millions and, in the case of the potato, became a key driver of nutrition and population growth despite farmers' initial reluctance.

Now listen, I'll admit that novelty is, on its own, pointless, but its impact can be globally life-enhancing. The post-script to the potato story arrived in 1845 when culinary neophilia had faded and, comfortable in the arms of the staple potato variety, much of Europe was planted with the same variety which was vulnerable to Phytophthora infestans (potato blight). In western Ireland the devastation it wreaked (worsened in many ways by the British) became known as the Irish Potato Famine, wiping out 1 million and forcing 1 million more to emigrate. We need to continue evolving and adapting our food and our diets to sustain the planet's population in a way that doesn't create an untenable burden on existing resources, and exploring new food sources is integral to that.

Entomophagy may well be one of the big answers to the world's food problems and while it is still in its infancy (at least in the west), it does offer huge prospects both in nutritional terms and for its low ecological impact. Unless we explore the potential of these foods, we will never know.

THE SCIENCE OF ENTOMOLOGY

I have a lovely tame entomologist called Sally-Ann Spence (she's not very tame at all, truth be told) who helped enormously with this book and she has asked me to explain to you what she does. Entomology is the scientific study of insects, and an entomologist is a person who studies them. It's essentially a branch of zoology and can relate to various aspects such as their social behavior, interaction with humans and their environments. It's a fascinating science, and you get to play with beautiful creatures. Sally-Ann showed me some of Charles Darwin's very own insects held in the glorious Oxford University Museum of Natural History.

Entomologists are often to be found not on the end of the phone when you need them, but away in absurdly glamorous tropical locations dragging some poor Coleoptera out of a tree for a chat. The other thing you need to know about entomologists is that although they are invariably bright and funny people, they are often a little grumpy about the amount of attention and resources lavished upon other branches of zoology whose combined biomass weight is a fraction of that of insects. Specifically 'bloody pandas and polar bears'. And don't try to reason with them about relative levels of cuteness – entomologists simply have a different brain for this kind of thing. Also entomologists can nip out into the back garden to get a fix of their favourite subject, unlike polar bear researchers, who need to wrap up warm and head north. Entomologists have a very dry sense of humour, and Sally-Ann takes great pride in the fact that her research project is the Dung Beetle UK Mapping Project, otherwise known as DUMP.

AUTHORS' NOTE: MY JOURNEY INTO ENTOMOPHAGY

I have been drawn to culinary adventure since my university days, but insects weren't on my radar until 16 years ago when I discovered *Why Not Eat Insects?* It's a small book – almost a pamphlet – written in 1885 by the nutty Victorian entomophagist Vincent Holt. Sadly Vince wasn't much cop as a chef and his recipe for slug soup is a particularly low point in the culinary canon. But his enthusiasm is infectious and the book lit a fire of culinary inquisitiveness that led me to cook my first London woodlouse cocktail and write *Gastronaut,* a wildly unpublishable book about strange and wonderful food adventures.

Soon after that book was, for various strange and wonderful reasons, published, I found myself travelling the world making TV programmes about culinary adventures of a more dangerous bent, specifically *Cooking in the Danger Zone,* which found me investigating conflict and extreme poverty seen through the prism of food. It led me to rebel-held Burma where we survived on cat, rotten fish and, finally, my first plate of bamboo grubs. Strange though they looked, the taste was phenomenal – an inulin-like sweetness (comparable to Jerusalem artichokes), combined with a deep umami richness from their high protein content. These weren't poverty foods by any stretch – they were a huge treat, served with grace and gravity by my host, and from that moment on I was a committed entomophagist.

Obviously, if your first experience of insect-eating is positive, things are looking up: this is food that challenges your fundamental sense of what's decent to eat, what's edible and what's not, food that makes you think about every mouthful, that combines elemental fear and heartwarming flavour. Food that makes you feel truly alive in a way that a chicken nugget never could.

I was on a roll: ugly-delicious palm weevils in Cameroon followed, as did bizarre, huge Colombian fat-arsed ants, and I delighted in the fact that they were both challenging and delicious. There's something strangely uplifting about overcoming latent disgust in order to eat your lunch, perhaps in the same way that heading out for a freezing cold winter run begins as torture and ends in ecstasy. Or is that just me? The point is that when I push myself into any culinary adventure my sensory perception is supercharged, and mere mouthfuls of food become memorable and fascinating.

My fascination with entomophagy melded inexorably into my writing and TV work as I featured them in documentaries and coaxed kids to eat them in children's shows with remarkable (and unexpected) success. Incidentally, kids are often much more open-minded about eating bugs than adults, but there's a technique: make sure that the first kid you offer the cricket to is the alpha child of the pack and (preferably) that they want to impress you with their bravery. When tackling a scary or unusual situation kids are trenchantly tribal and will follow their peer pack from the top down. Tell the first kid how brave they are to even pick the food up then taste it alongside them to celebrate their awesome awesomeness. Their peers will invariably follow. As it happens, both Daisy Gates (14) and Poppy Gates (12) have a clear preference for Mexican fly eggs. Not for the taste – they just like the texture.

Then, in 2010, insect eating seemed to come alive. Firstly, I convinced Richard Klein, the wonderful head of the quirky, erudite BBC4 TV channel, to commission a documentary called *Can Eating Insects Save the World?* Oh happy day. Together with my lovely producer Kari and cameraman Nik we headed to South-East Asia and tried delicious deep-fried grasshoppers, practically inedible giant water bugs, crickets, worms, tarantulas, and vicious biting red ants straight from the tree. At the same time, insect foods began to hit the market, and the press featured endless shock-horror stories about new products. It didn't quite feel that we had opened the entomophagy flood gates – but it certainly seemed that we had loosened the jar-lid.

So what next? I'd be kidding myself if I said that people are now embracing entomophagy with open arms. There is still a fair amount of gimmickry and novelty, but at least the subject now has broad awareness and a place in the media. The next stage is going to be much harder: transforming gimmicks into mouthfuls on a significant scale. On the whole my fellow Westerner most certainly does not share the fizz and tingle I get from culinary adventure. On the contrary they resort to type, they are neophobic, viewing culinary adventure as both pretentious and unnecessary, and are happy in the misconception that 'traditional is always best'. My work is ongoing, and so I must put faith in mankind's enlightened self-interest and its need to feed itself more efficiently – and cross my fingers that the potato paradigm is still relevant 500 years later!

DANGERS OF ENTOMOPHAGY

1. Don't eat any arthropods including insects, spiders and woodlice if you are allergic to shellfish, chocolate or house dust. In common with many protein-rich foods some arthropods are thought to trigger allergic reactions, and it's probably best for allergen sufferers to stay safe, pack this adventure away and climb a mountain instead. It's not clear what the triggers are but fingers point at the polysaccharide concentration in insects' chitinous exoskeletons, which can be similar to that in crabs, prawns and lobsters (it's complicated as chitin can actually help the immune system at certain levels). It may also block uptake of calcium. Similarly, if you have an allergic reaction to bee or wasp stings, it wouldn't be wise to eat their larvae or pupae. They can also contain pollen, so anyone suffering from bad hay fever might want to steer clear.

2. Don't be reckless. I will admit to having unthinkingly eaten some ridiculously dangerous animals in the past, partly because I'm a feckless greedy neophile and partly because people dared me to. These people fall into two camps: 1. People who are pointing a TV camera at me. 2. My daughters, Daisy and Poppy, who invariably dare me to eat whichever spider or fly may be passing. It's pathetic really: I've always found it impossible to dodge a dare. I have been lucky thus far and my metabolism may have been strengthened by tackling some of the filthiest, weirdest food on earth, but you don't need to demean yourself similarly. If it looks angry, spiky, ill or clearly designed by Beelzebub himself, don't eat it without consulting this book *and* asking a local who's eaten it before.

Here are a few specific dangers:

- Insects with *aposematic colouration* (loosely defined as 'looking scary to broadcast their unpalatability') may well contain bitter-tasting chemicals and should be avoided. These include ladybirds, tiger moth and cinnabar caterpillars (toxic due to chemicals gained from ragwort, its food plant).

- Mimicry, where one harmless insect mimics one that is not. Many species of hoverflies mimic wasps, for example. If you are unsure always avoid.

- False widow spiders have been known to give a painful bite. Wasps, bees, hornets and ants are capable of giving a painful sting. They may not be fatal stings in themselves, but you may get an allergic reaction to the venom that results in anaphylactic shock – and this can be fatal.

- Ticks can carry Lyme disease and hairy caterpillars should generally be avoided – especially the Oak processionary moth caterpillar that can cause serious skin rashes.

- Invertebrates that are listed as 'biters' include bed bugs, horseflies, midges, gnats, fleas, head and pubic lice, and mosquitoes. Be careful with them. Especially the pubic lice.

3. Always seek local advice. Species differ from region to region, with some safe to eat and others possibly toxic. You *must* ask for advice. Locals should know if pesticides and herbicides have been used in the area, potentially making your lunch toxic, too.

4. Tackle germs. Insects, like all foods, can harbour micro-organisms, from bacteria to tiny fungi. Correct handling and cooking is essential to get rid of potential pathogens. Some insects can be eaten whole but others, like the mopane worm eaten across Africa, need to be gutted: just give to them a really good squeeze so that their guts squirt out. Seems to do the trick nicely. And it goes without saying that your insects they should be cooked as thoroughly as any other meat product to ensure they are rid of any pathogens. Contamination from micro-organisms in properly dried insects shouldn't be a problem for consumers. The insects available commercially in the UK are mostly freeze-dried after being denied food for a day, which makes them safe if stored in cool, dry conditions. Alternatively, acidifying insects seems to work well as a preservative (in much the same way as sliced apple is tossed in citric acid to stop it going brown).

5. Beware of toxins. Some species of insect are, of course, dangerous to humans when alive, as are other arthropods such as tarantulas and scorpions. Most toxins are neutralised by cooking, but you must take local advice. Some caterpillars have poisonous spines on them that need to be burnt off before they are safe to eat, and the bogong moth of Australia isn't actually poisonous, but tests on the waste that vast groups leave on cave floors have shown large quantities of arsenic, potentially from pesticides. So consume in moderation. Studies have shown that insects caught in fields are far more likely to contain pesticides or heavy metals than those caught in dense forests.

6. Choking and other hazards. When you buy cooked Mexican chappulines or Thai grasshoppers, you may ask yourself 'where are their big grasshopper legs, for crying out loud?' Good question. They've been removed for your safety. Many species of grasshopper have legs with little backwards-facing barbs (much like an arrow) covered in spikes that can catch in your throat, causing a genuine choking hazard. It's even possible that they get stuck in your gut, possibly causing constipation, and have to be removed through surgery. Snap them off before eating.

7. Be kind to the environment and yourself. Collecting insects is great fun, but do be careful out there amidst all that wildlife because wandering through tarantula-infested fields, wasp-drenched forests and snake-soaked badlands is not for the faint-hearted. Be aware of the environmental dangers wherever you are, wear ankle-high boots, appropriate clothing, take a knowledgeable guide with you and listen to them. And be kind to the other inhabitants of your hunting grounds: birds, mammals and vegetation. Don't cut trees down to access a nest and check that your quarry isn't on the CITES list or endangered locally. There are also occasional instances of overharvesting – especially in areas where insect collecting provides big profits, as with mopane worms and some tarantulas. The point about entomophagy is to spread the ecological load attached to fulfilling our nutritional needs rather than cause new pressures.

When foraging, please be careful where you wander: avoid areas where pesticides have been applied and avoid nature reserves and SSSIs (Sites of Special Scientific Interest) etc. You may need to obtain a collecting licence in certain areas and unless the land on which you forage is clearly open to the public you should always seek the landowner's permission.

BENEFITS OF INSECT EATING

The ecological ramifications of entomophagy are hugely exciting. If we sourced at least some of our protein consumption from insects, we could alleviate a lot of pressure on the environment, for several reasons. Statistics in this area are a little patchy and hard to compare, but there's a clear pattern:

1. Feed . Insects are very efficient at using the planet's resources. Global livestock farming removes a vast proportion of the world's grain supply from the market to use as feed, and the most popular meats are relatively wasteful in comparison to insects. Crickets, on the other hand, convert food to protein very efficiently: it takes as little as 1.7kg of feed to produce 1kg of live crickets (of which the whole cricket is edible), and that feed is often waste matter. In order to produce protein insects use half as much feed as chickens and pigs, four times less than sheep and a whopping 12 times less than cattle.

2. *Greenhouse gas and ammonia emissions.* Insects are relatively kind to the environment. The livestock industry produces 7.1 gigatonnes of CO_2-equivalent emissions every year – that's 14% of all anthropogenic emissions – but it also produces 44% of all anthropogenic methane emissions (and methane is a particularly powerful greenhouse gas). That's partly because cows are ruminants, each producing around 600 litres of gas every day as they ferment food using bacteria from their rumen, and around 30 litres of that is methane. Multiply that by the lifespan of the average beef cow and you get 16,500-21,000 litres of methane *per cow*. That's a lot of methane. Greenhouse gas emissions of mealworms, crickets and locusts are lower by a factor of 100 when compared to beef and pork production, and very few insects produce any methane at all (with the exception of cockroaches and termites). Ammonia production is also much lower in insects, with pigs producing around 10 times as much per kilo of weight gain.

3. *Water (and land).* Water usage is becoming a crucial issue as climate change disrupts farming. Water-stress is already causing conflict in many areas, as is the availability of arable land when livestock production takes up 70% of all agricultural land use. This creates huge human and environmental pressures as land use and the water extracted (for growing the grain that is then fed to livestock) causes a concentration of embedded (or 'virtual') water use so great that it takes 22,000 litres of water to create 1kg beef. Statistics on water and land usage by insect farming are few and far between, but there seems little doubt that the lower feed:protein ratio leaves insects a vastly more efficient protein source, and the attendant land usage so much lower.

NUTRITIONAL BENEFITS

Bugs have been on the menu for many years contributing happily to a balanced diet but nutritional information is only just beginning to emerge. This is an a new area of nutritional research so data is still thin on the ground, but this much we know:

- Generally insects are very high in protein and many insect-protein products are beginning to appear on the shelves, including energy bars and products marketed to the weight-lifting community.

- Insects are also an excellent source of fat, including essential fatty acids such as the omega range (more commonly found in certain types of fish) and are important for a huge variety of organs from brains to bones.

- Insects are also packed with micronutrients (minerals, vitamins and their ilk) and invariably offer a rich source of iron, zinc, potassium, magnesium and sodium which are essential to a healthy diet.

BENEFITS FOR FARMERS AND FORAGERS

There is a clear interdependency between the insect forager and the field-owning farmer. When a team of grasshopper-hunters clears your fields of the hungry little fellas, there will be a short-term dip in the amount of your crop that disappears and that can only be a good thing for your rice harvest. The effect on the overall biomass will be insignificant due to the sheer number of the little beasts, and hunters will invariably leave the vast majority of insects behind hidden under the foliage, but it's better than nothing.

Insect *farming*, on the other hand, is a burgeoning new business and offers opportunities for those without an acre of land on which to graze a lovely big cow. There are around 20,000 cricket farms in Thailand, and in North America and Europe small-scale insect farms are beginning to crop up. Insect farms have long met the demand for pet reptile and bird food, and it's a short-ish leap to convert these to human food production. One of the many advantages of insects is they are very small and pretty easy to manage, enjoying close proximity. They don't ask for much to eat compared to larger mammals as they tend to metabolise food very efficiently (warm-blooded mammals waste a fair amount on heat generation). They are easily transportable, tend to breed like the clappers, and what they do eat is often waste matter such as wheat chaff. One problem with large-scale insect farming is the risk of catastrophic population collapse, often for no immediately apparent reason, so there is much work to be done to support the industry.

Foraging is often an important source of income for those living in poor rural areas. Women and children traditionally collect the mopane worm across Southern Africa, and although most insects are collected for personal consumption extras are often sold by women at local markets for a good price. In the West, edible insects are still sold largely as a novelty – chocolate-covered locusts, scorpions in lollipops and their ilk. As such, prices remain high and will continue to do so until demand increases.

THE FUTURE

So, do I think that people will all race to chow down on mealworm bolognaise and cricket pasta? Will Granny be scoffing grasshopper pie next Christmas?

No.

Not yet.

Futuregazing is a fool's game but it's a game that this particular fool is willing to play, so here goes: I believe that entomophagy will form several strands. Over the coming years foraging for insects in North America and Europe will grow in popularity in much the same way that we are reawakening to the joys of mushrooming and hedgerow cooking. It will be small-scale yet fundamentally important, as it will serve to fuel the discussion.

A small but noisy industry has developed over the last few years producing everything from fun Hallowe'en party food to insect protein bars and cricket-flour-fortified pasta. Restaurateurs and food developers are experimenting with insects, making snacks and tasters, incorporating them into fantastic dishes and enjoying a pleasing return of column inches for their effort. It has been a wave of fascination that many committed and talented people are riding while hoping that this will transform into a real industry with scale and infrastructure before their cash runs out.

While I'm hopeful that the major change they crave will come soon, I'm expecting to wait 20 years for the really big shift when people start eating insects on a significant scale. This is likely to come when ecological pressures have made traditional proteins too expensive or when people finally realise that they must change the way they drain the planet's resources or risk catastrophe. And that's when large-scale cricket and mealworm farming (not foraging) could fill the gap, producing protein that will be turned into burgers, sausages and pasta sauces. But of course those burgers and sausages won't be marketed with a photo of an insect on the packaging. In much the same way that Quorn packaging doesn't mention that it's made from fungus, mealworm burgers will accentuate the positive aspects and carry names like EarthBurger, EcoBurger, PlanetBurger or ForestBurger. They will carry pictures of happy polar bears (just to annoy the entomologists). The key factor is that they will be cheap. Sometimes we are driven by our wallets rather than our hearts and minds, so when the HappyPlanetBurger costs £1 compared to the beefburger's £10, we may finally have the makings of an eco-dietary revolution.

In the meantime, it's our duty to explore, and what a world there is to discover! My entomophagy escapades revealed to me a possible route from our ecologically and nutritionally disastrous monoculinary tendencies. But more importantly, they have led to extraordinary food adventures that have exmplained so much to me about the human condition and made my life worth living.

So hold on tight: let's do this thing.

UK AND
NORTHERN
EUROPE

You might think that the entomophagy-minded foodie would find slim pickings in northern Europe. After all, the region is colder than most, whereas insects thrive in warm climates. This can make insect-foraging a calorie-neutral or even calorie-negative endeavour, (whereby more energy is spent collecting your dinner than you gain from eating it). Much like munching on celery. And, yes, in terms of sheer number of species Europe ranks last in the league table of edible insects, with only 2% of the world's commonly eaten species.

But there are two counter-arguments to offer sceptics.

1. Insects are tenacious little critters and are found everywhere, especially in summer, as long as you know where to look and what to look for (and you have this book to hand). It's usually possible to walk into any garden that isn't under a blanket of snow and find a mouthful of protein.

2. The future of the world. Europe has always been at the forefront of global culinary endeavour, largely due to the work of the Dutch, who have been extracting food from an unpromising patch of mud since at least the Reformation. And with some degree of inevitability, they have thrown their weight behind entomophagy as an important solution to the world's food problems.

The Dutch are farming organic mealworms and crickets for human consumption, and the good folk at Wageningen University produce some brilliant entomophagy research. Big ideas that change global nutrition often sound a bit odd and distasteful at first. That doesn't mean we shouldn't try to change the world by changing what we eat.

THE MOST SURPRISING INSECT-BASED DISHES

Some of the most exciting developments in entomophagy have come from the most surprising places. Despite a climate that doesn't naturally lend itself to cold-blooded animals, northern Europe has developed a pleasing proportion of the world's oddest insect dishes. Check off the ones you've tried.

☐ *1. Bee mayonnaise*, Denmark.

☐ *2. Cockchafer soup*, France.

☐ *3. Fly burgers*, Malawi/Tanzania.

☐ *4. Mealworm ice cream*, San Francisco, USA.

☐ *5. Christmas minced flies*, London, UK.

(Admittedly, that last entry was one of your author's.)

MEADOW GRASSHOPPER

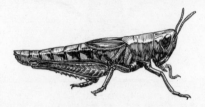

Chorthippus parallelus

The meadow grasshopper is known for its call; it attracts attention by rubbing its legs together and adding a scratchy noise to the general cacophony of a field on a summer's evening. The grasshopper is particularly good at hopping because its strong back legs act as tiny catapults – it bends its legs at the knee so that a spring-like mechanism stores up energy, then, when the grasshopper is ready to jump, it relaxes the leg muscles, allowing the spring to release and flinging it stylishly into the air. Despite this, they are very easy to catch when out in the open or on short grass, but in the middle of fields they invariably disappear into the vegetation, never to be seen again.

Taste: When freshly cooked they are crunchy and nutty with a strong umami hit.

Country: Found throughout the UK and much of Europe.

Habitat: In the wild the meadow grasshopper lives in damp pastures and meadows, spending its time merrily chirruping and feeding on leaves.

Dangers: They have no sting or venom and are no threat to humans.

How to cook/prep: Best roasted or deep-fried.

WATER BOATMAN

Corixidae

The water boatman spends its days leisurely rowing across ponds with its oar-like legs, eating algae and bits of vegetable detritus (which makes it unusual among its mostly carnivorous pond peers). But its most impressive skill is the ability to sing with its penis. Yes, you read that right: it's a penis-singer. It achieves this by rubbing the penis against its abdomen. The volume is spectacularly high, ranking as the loudest creature relative to its size. It has no teeth and instead dissolves its chosen morsel with its saliva before sucking up the resulting mush using its straw-like mouth. To survive underwater it has developed the ingenious technique of bringing a tiny air bubble under with it, tucked under its wing cases like a primitive scuba diver. Backswimmers (a similar species) are popular in Thailand and are eaten in soups or salted to make a dish known as *jom*. Water boatmen are also eaten in Mexico, both the adults and their eggs.

Taste: The eggs are quite the delicacy in Mexico, where they are known as 'Mexican caviar'. The adults on the other hand are slightly crablike.

Country: Widely spread throughout the UK.

Habitat: Happiest living their vegetarian existence in weedy ponds and rivers.

Dangers: Some species of backswimmer can bite, so do be careful.

How to cook/prep: Can be roasted, fried or boiled.

HIGHLAND MIDGES

Culicoides impunctatus

Although they have a tiny wingspan of 1mm, these are the most bloodthirsty of Scotland's 40 species of midge; the highland midge has a fearsome reputation as one of the UK's most annoying insects, scourge of camping trips and harbinger of itchy misery. The female of the species tends to be the one that goes for us and extracts her dinner by making minute cuts on our skin and then happily lapping away at the pool of blood. They release a chemical that stops the blood from clotting, meaning they can merrily gorge themselves before flying off and leaving us itchy and cross. Nobody is spared, even those of royal blood – Queen Victoria grumbled in her 1872 diary that she was 'half devoured' by the pests. In Africa midges are harvested and pressed into solid blocks called a *kunga* cake. It's time to turn the tables on our Scottish insects and do the same.

Taste: Slightly nutty and a little musty. Once mushed into a cake and then crumbled into food they add an umami richness (like Parmesan cheese taste without the cheesiness) to stews and soups.

Country: Widespread in north Wales and Scotland.

Habitat: Rarely if ever farmed – people generally try to avoid them. Your best chance of gathering a midge harvest would be going out at dusk or dawn with a very fine net and possibly a torch and using yourself as bait. Or copy the east African method of wetting a frying pan with oil so that the midges stick to it when waved through a swarm. This works remarkably well.

Dangers: None known.

How to cook/prep: Gather as many as you can and press them into a cake. Make burgers with it, or dry it out and grate parts of it off into stews.

GIANT HOUSE SPIDER

Eratigena atrica

The giant house spider isn't an insect, and it's not even *that* giant in the ranking of massive arachnids, generally reaching 18mm in body length (but with proportionally long legs – up to 75mm, in males). Despite having shared homes with humanity for millennia they are relatively shy, preferring to make their funnel-shaped webs in dark undisturbed places and then sit and wait for prey. Cushy job? Not really. From July to October the males can be seen prowling the house looking for a mate, but after spending a few delicious weeks with their main squeeze she usually eats him. The babies are called spiderlings, which makes them sound quite sweet – until you see around 60 emerging from each egg sac. They are one of the world's speediest spiders, managing to scuttle at speeds of up to 1.18 mph.

Taste: Let's be honest here: the eating experience is mainly crunch and funky-tasting juice, but there's a savoury protein punch from a plate of them, and when scattered with salt they make a wonderful snack.

Country: Very widely spread all across the UK.

Habitat: Happiest inside the home in quiet crannies where they have both access to lots of prey and isolation from meddlesome humans and their stinky pets.

Dangers: Like all spiders, they do produce venom to stun their prey but are unlikely to bite humans, much preferring to run away. The venom is invariably neutralised by cooking.

How to cook/prep: Wash, dry and deep-fry. Drain on paper, toss in salt and paprika and serve.

GREATER WAX MOTH LARVAE

Galleria mellonella

The greater wax moth's larvae, or waxworms, are a beekeeper's worst nightmare, gobbling away at impurities in the wax in honeybee hives and causing a huge amount of damage to the eventual honey yield. They can even eat the heads of bee pupae. But let's not damn them too early – the larvae are incredibly useful as pet feed and are also used in scientific experiments, not to mention being rather scrummy to humans. In their book *Entertaining With Insects, or: The Original Guide to Insect Cookery*, Ronald L. Taylor and Barbara J. Carter describe the larvae as 'thin-skinned, tender, and succulent. They would appear to lend themselves to commercial exploitation as snack items. When dropped into hot vegetable oil, the larvae immediately swell, elongate and then burst. The resulting product looks nothing like an insect, but rather like popcorn'. Just beware of chip-pan fires.

Taste: Often reared on a diet of bran and honey, when roasted or sautéed they taste like a cross between pine nuts and enoki mushrooms, but also very fatty.

Country: Found all over Europe.

Habitat: They are happy anywhere with an adequate supply of food, but the larvae really do love bees' nests. They are widely available commercially as food for geckos and other reptiles.

Dangers: Harmless if properly cooked.

How to cook/prep: Sautéed or roasted (after popping in the freezer for half an hour to send them to sleep).

BLACK SOLDIER FLY

Hermetia illucens

The black soldier fly tries to make itself look fearsome by pretending to be a wasp; it has opaque patches on its middle to give the appearance of the pinched waist of its distant stinging cousin. These flies make excellent eating as larvae (though you can eat the adults too). The larvae are a protein-rich (42% protein) dinner for all sorts of animals and are farmed for animal feed as they are highly efficient at converting vegetation to protein. And for humans? Well, a prototype tabletop domestic farm contraption created by an Austrian designer managed to breed 500g of larvae for human consumption in two weeks. They are industrious little things, adept at breaking down waste into compost and highly efficient at reproducing from a small amount of food. They can even thrive on human faeces (which doesn't sound particularly appealing). You can often spot them lurking around cowpats, but in fact the adults have no functioning mouth – they spend their time searching for mates, not eating.

Taste: When cooked the larvae smell like potatoes and the taste is nutty and meaty.

Country: Found throughout the UK.

Habitat: Nooks and crannies around decomposing waste and manure. They are hard to forage on any sort of scale – you really need to catch a few adults to start a domestic larvae farm colony. There is a commercial market for these flies (for fish and pet food and animal feed), for which they are grown in huge tanks called worm bins.

Dangers: They have no sting or venom and are no threat to humans.

How to cook/prep: Roast or stir-fry.

BLACK GARDEN ANT

Lasius niger

The most common variety of ant found in the UK, these are ingenious insects with a complex hierarchy and interesting behaviour. They usually farm certain species of aphid, offering them protection in exchange for a sugary secretion the aphids give off called honeydew, which the ants find utterly delicious. The worker ants are often found swarming around soft fruits and other sweet things and are all female, numbering around 5,000 per colony. The lazy males don't work and are only produced for the flying season when they and the young virgin queens of the species take their magnificent nuptial flight to form new colonies, where the queens can live for a whopping 15 years. The males are less lucky, dropping dead a few days after landing.

Taste: The adults taste pleasantly zesty as they, like many ants, contain formic acid (from the Latin word for ant, 'formica') for use as a defence mechanism when threatened. Their light crunchy texture is satisfyingly toothsome.

Country: Widespread across the UK, northern Europe and parts of north America and Asia.

Habitat: A queen can make a new nest anywhere, from ordinary soil to cracks in pavements. The worker ants can be found far and wide as they explore extensively during the summer months to look for new food supplies. It's easy to catch them by offering something sweet such as a piece of fruit, and shaking them off it into a container.

Dangers: *Lasius niger* are harmless and will be safe to eat after roasting.

How to cook/prep: Best eaten simply roasted with salt.

SPECKLED BUSH CRICKET

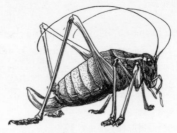

Leptophyes punctatissima

Crickets are an immensely popular snack across the world as they are easy to catch (most of them don't jump particularly well) and enormously nutritious.

These ones are easily found in the British countryside. The females have a special tube for depositing eggs called an ovipositor, which looks a little like a scimitar, while both sexes are covered in the very dashing little black spots that give them their name. Both are flightless but extremely agile, bouncing around using their long slender back legs. Many species are also very easy to farm, which is why there are around 20,000 cricket farms in Thailand. If you need to cure yourself of entomophobia, I recommend putting your arms into a cricket farm box (about the size of a kitchen table) and letting them run all over you. Bracing stuff.

Taste: When eaten freshly fried, they are crispy and meaty (due to their high protein content), like a cross between ready salted crisps and roast chicken. Dried, they have a nutty taste, and can be rehydrated in soy sauce and stock for extra depth.

Country: Most commonly found in south and central England and the Welsh coast.

Habitat: They are mostly nocturnal and are found in many different habitats. In the UK, they are easy to find in fields, grassland and meadows. Use a head-torch at night-time or hang up a white sheet in the garden and point a bright light as it. You should find them quite easily.

Dangers: None known.

How to cook/prep: Dispatch them by dropping them into water, and then shake dry before deep-frying them in hot sunflower oil for 3–7 minutes, depending on size, and testing them after three minutes. Toss them in salt and eat them as a snack.

SESAME CRICKET NIBBLES

Ingredients
500ml groundnut oil for deep frying
50g dried crickets
2 tbsp soy sauce
1 tbsp mirin (or 1 tbsp caster sugar)
2 tbsp white sesame seeds

Method
- Heat your oil to 180°C (350°F/Gas Mark 4).

- Fry your crickets in batches for 30 seconds at a time, then place on kitchen paper to soak up the excess oil.

- Mix the soy sauce with the mirin or sugar and dip your crickets in the mix.

- Roll the crickets in the white sesame seeds and serve.

COMMON COCKCHAFER

Melolontha melolontha

Although this insect finds itself in possession of a silly name, it still manages to have a rich set of even sillier pseudonyms including 'billy witch'. The common cockchafer is distinguished by its fabulous antler-like antennae – the boys have seven 'leaves' while the girls only have six. The cockchafer larva spends years underground scoffing roots and was considered troublesome by farmers before the widespread use of pesticides. Cockchafer larvae were actually put on trial in 1320s Avignon, France, and sentenced to exile in a special reserve. Perhaps unsurprisingly, they didn't pay much heed to this decree. They even lent one of their nicknames, 'doodlebug', to Germany's V-1 rocket because of the loud buzzing the bombs made during flight.

Although they were nearly eradicated in the middle of the twentieth century, there are currently no pesticides approved for use against them, and as their numbers are increasing they are once again considered a pest so, on balance, it's fair to suggest restrained consumption.

Taste: Both the larvae and the adult beetles are considered a bit of a delicacy and can be found in a wide number of European recipes. The larvae and beetles are rich, meaty and sometimes slightly shrimp-like.

Country: Found all across the UK but in particular in the south of England, as well as mainland Europe.

Habitat: The larvae live underground eating tubers for up to three years, and emerge in spring for a glorious six weeks of mating and leaf-eating. Unfortunately for farmers, cereal fields make an ideal breeding ground for them.

Dangers: Harmless if properly cooked.

How to cook/prep: As well as the delicious recipe given below, they can also be roasted in butter, then covered in a dusting of sugar.

COCKCHAFER SOUP

Ingredients
3 tbsp butter
50g adult cockchafers, wings and legs removed
500ml chicken stock
The meat from two roast chicken legs, shredded
200g oyster mushrooms, torn into pieces
Dash of double cream
Chopped parsley
Chopped chives
Toasted sourdough bread

Method
- Heat 2 tbsp of the butter in a wide frying pan until sizzling and add the cockchafers. Cook until golden and set aside on some kitchen paper to dry.

- Heat the stock in a saucepan and mix in the meat from the chicken legs, then simmer on a low heat until bubbling.

- Add the remaining butter to the frying pan and fry the mushrooms until golden-tinged. Add them to the stock with the cockchafers.

- Stir in the double cream, season the soup and sprinkle with the herbs. Serve with toasted bread.

EARTHWORMS

Several species in the class *Oligochaeta*

Not actually an insect but nonetheless one of the most fascinating creatures on earth, the slimy, hermaphroditic, mucus-covered earthworm has no eyes (although it does possess some photosensitive cells on its back and sides), nose or ears. In fact, the best way to tell the front from the back is to observe which way it's going. It does, however, have lots of taste receptors all over its body – especially towards the head, which contains its mouth, positioned just under the tip of its snout. There's also an excellent set of microscopic bristles (four to each segment of the worm) that help it to move, and also provide some traction for it to resist the pull of a hungry bird. When mature it also has a 'saddle', called a clitellum, which it uses to mate with. Earthworms are big business, bred to help decompose food waste, but rarely farmed for food. The Maori in New Zealand have been known to eat them; they call them *noke*.

Taste: Squidgy and protein-ey, they occasionally have a disarmingly strong lingering sweetness similar to Thai bamboo caterpillars – the same sugary sensation you find in Jerusalem artichokes.

Country: Found worldwide.

Habitat: In the ground.

Dangers: None known, but be very careful that they haven't been feeding on pesticide- or insecticide-treated land.

How to cook/prep: Purge for several days, as with snails. Then stir-fry.

COMMON WOODLOUSE

Oniscus asellus

A wondrous minibeast mouthful, woodlice are terrestrial isopod crustaceans related to shrimp, part of the 5,000-strong suborder of *Oniscidea* and, like earthworms, not actually insects at all; but they are similarly in the right zone for this book. Small, sociable and prehistoric-looking, they have a rigid exoskeleton broken down into segments, and 14 jointed limbs. They feed mostly on dead plant matter and prefer damp environments as they excrete water rapidly. Some of them can roll up into a perfect sphere. They don't spread disease and despite their name they don't damage sound wood. They are known as 'cheesy bobs' in Guildford, and 'chiggy pigs' in north Devon, which shows that (unusually for the creatures in this book) some people find them rather cute.

Taste: Slight crabbiness or shrimpiness, probably due to their close relationship to sea shrimp. They have nice crunchy exoskeletons and the sweet meat delivers a delightful burst of umami when sympathetically cooked.

Country: Very widespread – they thrive in the UK and many other countries across the world.

Habitat: Never found in shops, so you'll have to catch your own. Luckily, they are easily foraged in the UK throughout the year – rotting logs are the most common place to discover them. Carefully shift your log and move fast to gather them up into a tub before they can hide again.

Dangers: As long as you boil them gently before eating, they pose no danger as the short boil will kill most pathogens from the soil. Don't eat if you are allergic to shellfish.

How to cook/prep: Rinse them briefly, pop them into boiling water and cook for 60 seconds, then drain/dry them off. They are an excellent substitute for shrimps in a prawn cocktail or on their own as a grub nibble, cooked and sprinkled with smoked paprika.

WOODLOUSE PRAWN COCKTAIL

(serves 2)

Ingredients
50g woodlice (if you gather more, adjust the below quantities accordingly)
2 tbsp tomato ketchup
2 tbsp mayonnaise
Dash of Tabasco
Dash of lemon juice
Dash of Worcester sauce
1 x Little Gem lettuce, separated, washed and dried
Cayenne pepper to garnish

Method
- Blanch your woodlice in boiling, salted water until cooked (around two minutes), then set aside to drain in a sieve.

- Place all the wet ingredients in a bowl and stir to mix. This is your Marie Rose sauce.

- Take two bowls and place half the lettuce leaves into each.

- Spoon half of the Marie Rose sauce onto the lettuce in each bowl.

- Share the cooked woodlice out between the bowls, sprinkle with cayenne pepper and serve.

MEALWORMS

Tenebrio molitor

The larvae of the darkling beetle, *Tenebrio molitor*, mealworms are some of the most easily available edible insects in the west, not because they are found in great numbers in the wild but because they are easily farmed. Although most farms still produce them for bird feed and as live insect feed for reptiles, some are producing the same larvae for human consumption. They are sometimes found as fake tequila worms, left ignobly to sit in cheap brands of tequila – the real tequila worm used in some types of mescal is actually the larvae of the moth *Hypopta agavis*. The female darkling beetle lays up to 500 eggs in one go, making mealworms easy and profitable to farm on a commercial level. Strangely enough, mealworms can eat polystyrene, converting it into usable organic matter.

Taste: Slightly mushroomy, nutty and a little bitter, but they tend to take on the flavours of whatever you cook them with.

Country: Widely spread across the world.

Habitat: In the wild they like dark, safe areas where lots of rotting is going on. They can be found wriggling their way through stored grains, but are happy eating everything from oats to apples.

Dangers: None known.

How to cook/prep: They can be added to healthy shakes as they are an excellent source of protein. Try roasting for a crunchy, flavourful topping that goes particularly well with avocado.

MEALWORM BOLOGNESE

(serves 2)

Ingredients
50g dried mealworms
300ml chicken or vegetable stock
Pinch of mixed herbs
2 tbsp olive oil
1 onion, finely chopped
Sunflower oil
2 garlic cloves
1 tin chopped plum tomatoes

Method
- Soak your mealworms in 100ml of the stock, herbs and olive oil for 30 minutes, then drain off any excess liquid and whizz them up in a food processor.

- Gently fry the onion in a splash of sunflower oil for five minutes, add the mealworms and crushed garlic and fry for another five minutes.

- Add the tomatoes and the rest of the stock and simmer very gently for another 20 minutes or so.

- Add the sauce to some cooked pasta and enjoy with Parmesan.

MY TOP 5 EDIBLE INSECT STOCKISTS

If you can't find enough tasty critters in your own backyard, there are plenty of places that provide grubstock to satisfy your culinary curiosity. Here's my list of the best UK suppliers:

Eat Grub – selling sustainably sourced insects in both their raw form for your own cooking as well as in a range of delicious snack bars
http://www.eatgrub.co.uk/

Crunchy Critters – for all your dehydrated and freeze-dried edible insect needs. They also provide Bush Tucker Banquets which are perfect for scaring squeamish guests at dinner parties.
https://www.crunchycritters.com/

Crobar – you'll be seeing these snazzy looking snack bars popping up at a health food shop near you soon enough. In the meantime you can by their cricket flour based snacks online.
http://gathrfoods.com/

Jimini's – Only the French could embrace insects as a perfect accompaniment to wine and Champagne. That's exactly what Jimini's have done and their bar-snack alternatives to run of the mill peanuts are available at Fortnum & Mason's as well as online.
https://www.jiminis.com/

Your local pet food shop- if its good enough for your pet reptile its good enough for you. Pet food shops are an easy place to pick up insects in bulk: an ideal way to kick-start your very own insect farm!

SOUTHERN
EUROPE

Southern Europe has a lusty enthusiasm for entomophagy in its classical literature, from Herodotus' reports of the Nasamones' 'hunt for locusts' to Aristophanes' poulterers who sold 'four-winged fowl' (probably grasshoppers). Pliny the Elder mentions *Cossus cossus*, the larvae of the goat moth, considered by ancient Romans to be a great delicacy. What a pity, then, that Europe now shares a rich-world aversion to eating insects. That doesn't mean, however, that they, like the rest of the unsuspecting world, don't eat them all the time. E120 is a prime example: the cochineal insect gives up its deep red carminic acid to dye anything from sweets to sausages. And let's face it, if more Southern Europeans were aware that they are spreading multiply regurgitated bee vomit on their toast whenever they have honey for breakfast, perhaps overt entomophagy would seem less of a giant leap.

TOP 5 MOST SURPRISING INSECT PRODUCTS

Seeing as the ancient Greeks and Romans were such enthusiastic entomophagists it's no surprise that some of the weirdest insect products (including Spanish fly and Cochineal) have been produced in Southern Europe. What's particularly exciting is that the public has tended to ignore the insect connection of late – perhaps through horror, perhaps embarrassment. Let's put a stop to that. Tick off the ones you've (possibly unknowingly) tried:

- ❏ *1. Spanish Fly.* An aphrodisiac (well, it's actually a urogenital-tract irritant, highly dangerous – even fatal – if taken in high doses). It's made from the emerald-green *Lytta vesicatoria* beetle.

- ❏ *2. Cochineal insects.* Food dye E120.

- ❏ *3. Shellac.* Insect excreta. Food glaze E904.

- ❏ *4. Honey.* Multiple-regurgitated bee vomit.

- ❏ *5. Propolis.* 'Bee glue' holistic antibiotic (popular in health stores but only rated as 'possibly effective' for treating genital herpes and cold sores).

CHEESE MITES

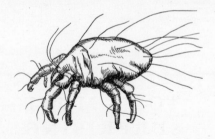

Acarus siro

Only just visible to the naked eye, these cheeky little (0.33–0.66mm) beasts are intentionally introduced into some cheeses to develop their flavour and appearance. French Mimolette and some vintage Vieux Cantal cheesemakers use them and if you buy the cheese in French markets you can sometimes see the mites on the surface (I have spotted them several times at Gignac market in the Languedoc region). They munch away at the rind, causing damage that leaves behind an interesting texture, increases pungency and gives that all-important impression of age. Wondrous though they are in cheese, they are a pest in flour and grain, causing farmers a multitude of woes. Interestingly, the German Milbenkäse cheese uses a different type of mite called *Tyrophagus casei*.

Taste: Impossible to tell what the mites themselves taste of as they are so tiny, but the cheeses they live on are rendered pungent and heady. In the case of Vieux Cantal, this can be taken to the level of farmyard effluent (in a good way).

Country: They are a pest across the world, but in cheese they are mainly used in France.

Habitat: Cheese.

Dangers: None. Unless you're an animal continually eating infested feed, in which case you can get intestinal inflammation and diarrhoea.

How to cook/prep: If you find them in your cheese, rejoice. You've bought a fine slab of dairy that's been made with love. The mites don't need to be removed and you should go ahead and eat them.

JUNE BEETLE

Amphimallon pini

A pretty little beetle of the same family as the noble scarab that rolled the sun across the sky in Egyptian mythology. The name 'June beetle' in fact applies to a whole range of subspecies, all rich in folklore. They are usually around 20mm long, and tend to emerge as beetles in balmy spring weather after three or so years lurking underground, as white grubs, eating roots. These grubs are the bane of gardeners up and down the country due to their plant-destroying capabilities. During their time flying around treetops looking for potential romantic encounters they get attracted to lights, which explains their tenacious attraction to your bedroom window. For this reason they generally aren't regarded as the sharpest tools in the shed; in 1922 F. H. Chittendon wrote that the green June beetle, 'appeared to be utterly unaware of their danger and are as stupid as the *Scarabaeidae* are generally accredited with being, at least when not in flight'.

Taste: Buttery and walnutty.

Country: Across southern Europe.

Habitat: They adore lawns, hedgerows, anywhere with lots of food.

Dangers: They should be properly cleaned and cooked before eating, as with all insects.

How to cook/prep: Remove legs and wings, then take a leaf from the Native Americans: roast them on hot coals.

MAYFLIES

Ephemeroptera

Mayflies, also known as shadflies, are an ancient insect closely related to the dragonfly. They have long intrigued humanity, perhaps because of their ephemeral nature: swarms of giant (13cm) hatching mayflies are a tourist attraction in Hungary, where their breeding activities are known as the 'Tisza Blooming'; they erupt from the water to mate, only to perish a few hours later. Even Aristotle found time to talk about the mayfly, and in 1785 George Crabbe compared their fleeting existence to that of daily newspapers:

> *In shoals the hours their constant numbers bring*
> *Like insects waking to th' advancing spring;*
>
> *Which take their rise from grubs obscene that lie*
> *In shallow pools, or thence ascend the sky:*
> *Such are these base ephemeras, so born*
> *To die before the next revolving morn.*

These 'grubs obscene' have also been a great help to anglers, who have long used them as bait and fashioned artificial lures that resemble them. They are on the menu in north Vietnam, Japan and China, too.

Taste: They have a delicate soft crunch and taste like the base of a stem of grass. That said, they can sometimes smell a little musty.

Country: All over southern Europe.

Habitat: As nymphs they are found in streams under rocks or near decaying vegetation in ponds. As adults they emerge en masse from the water to fly around.

Dangers: None known.

How to cook/prep: They can be eaten raw (with the wings removed for ease of eating). Alternatively, if you are faced with a large number they can be squidged together to form a protein-rich cake.

EUROPEAN RED WOOD ANT

Formica rufa

Formic acid isn't, perhaps, the most mouthwatering condiment with which to souse your lunch, but the lovely zesty kiss of edible ants first came to the attention of science when they were collected in 1671 by John Ray, an English naturalist, to be crushed and distilled for their acid. These ants are feisty little critters with a penchant for spraying their acid at predators and other things that annoy them. They also deliver one of the more painful bites of the ant family, and can grow up to 1cm long.

Taste: Due to the acidity they have a pleasantly sour, citrusy taste. This is mixed with a sweetness from one of their principal sources of food – the honeydew secretion they harvest by stroking the backs of their farmed aphids.

Country: Not very common in the UK but found in many areas of Southern Europe.

Habitat: They like to make their nests in deciduous forests near pine trees, and use a natural resin that drips from trees as a sort of disinfectant. Their nests can reach heights of several metres.

Dangers: They can bite and spray painful acid, but are fine to eat when cooked.

How to cook/prep: Can be eaten raw, but perhaps best toasted or fried.

ROMAN SNAIL

Helix pomatia

Snails are so far removed from the insect world that they're in a different taxonomic solar system: that of the *Gastropoda*. But I've included the beautiful *Helix pomatia* because if you're brave enough for entomophagy, you'll take gastropophagy in your stride (or you're a gardener in search of vengeance). These snails reach a top speed of around 1.3cm/second and lay surprisingly large eggs (which can be eaten as 'snail caviar') that hatch after three to four weeks into the cutest tiny translucent baby snails with soft shells. Common throughout much of Europe, they must not be collected or killed in the wild in England, where they are a protected species, but can be farmed. Like all land snails they have four tentacles on their heads; the two longest ones have very simple eyes and all four are covered in taste buds. The tentacles have a wondrous ability to retract, turning themselves inside out like a rubber glove for protection.

Pretty much any snail is edible if you take a few precautions. The slime they create slows down the rate of moisture loss from the snail, but shouldn't stop you collecting them. Incidentally, slugs' slime is much thicker, making them impossible to transform into a decent snack. Believe me: I've tried.

Taste: Snails provide a solid nugget of juicy protein similar to an overcooked mussel with an extra earthiness. Cooked long and slow they are tender enough, but be careful – a shorter boil will leave you with a hunk of rubbery nonsense unworthy of your chemoreceptors.

Country: Collected and eaten across Europe, especially in France, where 700 million of them are eaten annually, cooked into multitudinous regional recipes. Remember: it's illegal to catch or kill them in England.

Habitat: Very widespread: gardens, canals, rivers, forests, open countryside.

Dangers: Snails must be purged before eating to rid them of any toxins, slug pellets or other nasties. As with flies, you don't know where they've been, so take care.

How to cook/prep: Keep them in a box for a week or so, fed on fresh salad or veg. Withdraw food for the last two to three days and then boil them for around two hours until tender. Garlic butter and parsley optional.

SEA SLATER

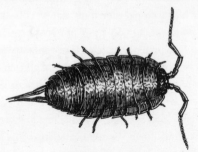

Ligia oceanica

This is not actually an insect but a fabulous relative of the woodlouse that lives in temperate water and grows up to 30mm long. It is undiscerningly omnivorous, happy eating seaweed, algae and just about any organic muck it finds that will fit into its mouth. Although they are nocturnal feeders, anyone who's enjoyed exploring the shoreline will have at some point disturbed and seen them. You'll find them while exploring the shoreline, clambering over rocks and pottering in rockpools looking for shrimps and crabs, but just as often ignored. It's a shame – they make great eating. Collect them together with your shrimps, mussels and assorted shoreline goodies, and poach together in seawater.

Taste: Shrimp-like: sweet umami-rich meat.

Country: Pretty much all temperate waters – across Europe down to the Mediterranean Sea and on the Atlantic coast of the USA.

Habitat: Rocky seashores, pools, under rocks and in cracks.

Dangers: None known.

How to cook/prep: Boil or steam and make into a sea slater cocktail (like a prawn cocktail).

SEA SLATER FRITTERS

(snacks for 4)

Ingredients
100g plain flour
1 egg yolk
50ml iced water
1 large courgette, grated
1 shallot, thinly sliced
50g sea slaters (or as many as you can collect), blanched
100ml vegetable oil (or enough to make a 1cm-deep pool in your pan)

Method

- Pour the flour into a large bowl and mix in the egg and water (this should be thick pancake consistency, so add more water if necessary), then season lightly.

- Add the courgettes and shallots to the batter, adding a pinch of salt, and then add the sea slaters. Form into several, roughly egg-sized, patties. Squash down to make little fritters.

- Fry until golden on both sides and cooked through.

- Serve with chopped parsley and a squeeze of lemon.

EUROPEAN MANTIS

Mantis religiosa

The praying mantis has become infamous over the years, perhaps due to the mating habit of the female (occasionally eating the head of the male after, or even during, sex) and the anthropomorphism with which we imbue them due to their piously-poised forelegs. Adding to the slightly sinister skill set, they have the uncanny ability to turn their heads through 180 degrees to scan their surroundings for movement. They have good sight but only one ear, located on their belly just forward of their hind legs. Lady mantises lay their eggs inside a protective sac that erupts with a profusion of tiny, perfectly formed mantises come springtime. Interestingly, the females seem to eat the males more frequently under lab conditions – perhaps out of boredom? They are also prone to decapitating their mates *before* mating. Call me old fashioned, but that's a bit creepy.

Taste: Slightly mushroomy and shrimpy.

Country: Found in temperate and tropical climates worldwide.

Habitat: On leaves, branches – anywhere they are likely to find prey.

Dangers: None known.

How to cook/prep: Remove the legs and fry.

CHEESE FLY MAGGOTS

Piophila casei

This fly is only 4mm long but, much like myself, it is fond of meat, fish and cheese. Unlike myself, though, it will happily lay its eggs among all of them. In most cases this is an unwelcome intrusion but in Sardinia and Corsica cheese fly larvae are intentionally introduced to help decompose cheese and develop its flavour. The cheese is called *casu marzu* in Sardinia and *casgiu merzu* in Corsica, and is revered or avoided depending on your propensity for culinary adventure. The maggots have an extraordinary ability to jump, hence their nicknames 'bacon skippers' and 'cheese hoppers'. They do this by curling up and grabbing hold of their rear ends, tensing their muscles to increase internal blood pressure, then letting go of their behinds. On release the pressure makes their bodies straighten almost instantly, forcing the maggot to jump up to 15cm into the air. Well, everyone needs a thing, don't they?

Taste: The cheese they create is visciously pungent. *Casu marzu* has a sour, astringent taste and an overwhelming smell of ammonia. The decomposition leads to extreme fermentation and a breakdown of the dairy fats, causing liquid to seep from it. Unless you are stout-hearted, it's perhaps an adventure to be enjoyed just the once, followed by a very large glass of wine and a hearty slap on the back.

Country: Sardinia (Italy) and Corsica (France).

Habitat: *Piophila casei* are found across most of the world.

Dangers: If you can stomach the cheese, you can stomach the maggots.

MEDITERRANEAN TERMITE

Reticulitermes lucifugus

In contrast to most insects, termites are to blame for a vast amount of global methane and CO2 emissions: 4% of the former and 2% of the latter. This particularly ugly sub-species is prevalent in southern France. The colonies of termites are exquisitely organised, with a complex hierarchy from workers up to soldiers and queens, living together in huge populations of many thousands. The sterile workers are left to the task of hunting and eating food (often nice dry wood that would otherwise have been really useful for propping up your house); they then regurgitate the fruits of their labours for the higher castes to eat. Delicious! The soldiers have vicious pincers on their heads that they use to squash invading ants, and the queens and flying varieties are left to the enviable task of frantic and focused reproduction. The diet of the termite is, however, a huge problem across the world, to the extent that termite control costs the US economy up to two billion dollars per year (although termite *damage* only costs half a billion dollars a year). In Malaysia, however, the 'if you can't beat 'em, eat 'em' philosophy has led to a vogue in eating the two-inch-long queen termites dipped in rice wine.

Taste: Hard and crunchy on the outside but soft and creamy within, slightly reminiscent of almonds. Raw termites can taste like fried whitebait and hazelnuts.

Country: They have, in recent years, made their way as far north as Devon, but generally are happiest in France and further south.

Habitat: Old, dry timbers and trees.

Dangers: As long as they are properly cooked they should pose no hygiene problems for adventurous eaters.

How to cook/prep: Similar to ants, they are best deep-fried or roasted with a little salt and oil. They are versatile – the Florida Pest Control website even has a recipe for termite and rice soup.

AFRICA

Africa is a treasure trove of unusual insect products from *kunga* cake (made from thousands of lake midges) to the extraordinary melon bug/sorghum bug oil mix that can be used as biodiesel for your car. But the continent is probably most famous for mopane worms and palm weevils; mopane worms because of the sheer scale of the harvest, and palm weevils because ... well, the day you buy your first bag of palm weevils (also known as sago grubs) is the day you win your insect-eating wings. Sink your teeth into one and you've crossed the entomophagic Rubicon. Those beasts are everything the timid eater fears: big, alien, unknowable, unfamiliar, ugly.

But then so is a lobster, and that's where the magic lies. Because once you get over entomophobia (which, admittedly, can take a few goes), these scary and unusual beasts can, if cooked well, taste absolutely fantastic. It's much the same with sheeps' eyeballs. They have a similar taste and texture to foie gras, but their reputation is hamstrung by the sheer horror of most people's reactions. So perhaps the squelch and tang and wriggle of the palm weevil just needs to become familiar to be enjoyed.

Generally speaking, there are fewer different species available at markets in Africa than in Asia, but foraging happens on such a scale that the sheer number of different types eaten is vast – 524 individual species across 36 countries, or 30% of the world's total.

5 CURRENT AND POTENTIAL USES OF INSECTS AS ANIMAL FEED

Africa has huge untapped global trading potential. One small route to prosperity could be in monetising its natural bounty of insects for use as animal feed, and why not? Many are already approved for use, and it's an emerging market that many developing countries could benefit from, lightening the load caused by the use of fish and animal protein for farmed animals:

1. *Black soldier flies.* Chicken/pig/prawn feed.

2. *Common housefly larvae or 'maggots'.* Chicken feed.

3. *Silkworms.* Chicken feed.

4. *Yellow mealworms.* Already used as chicken feed.

5. *Wild termites.* Fish bait.

MELON BUG OIL

Aspongopus vidiuatus
Also the sorghum bug *Agonoscelis pubescens*

Both the melon bug and the sorghum bug are Sudanese natives, They are considered pests, but they offer humans a bizarre and wonderful resource. When the 20mm-long adult melon bugs are soaked in hot water they render a nutritious oil called *um-buga* that's used for food and as a medicine to treat skin lesions (it has high antibacterial activity). It's similar in colour to sunflower oil and it's stable over long periods of time (it won't turn rancid like many animal fats). In faraway Namibia, the same adult bugs are ground into a powder and used as a spice. In Sudan the sorghum bug is similarly used as food and pressed; it packs a whopping 60% of yellowish oil (as opposed to the melon bug's 45% reddish oil). A wealth of serious research has been carried out into these insect oils, including promising work on its use as a biodiesel.

Taste: A pleasant, clean, sweet oil.

Country: Sudan.

Habitat: Infestations of watermelon and sorghum.

Dangers: None known.

How to cook/prep: Soak melon bugs in hot water and press. The oil should rise to the surface. Similarly, if you press the adult sorghum bug in water it will release oil that can be collected and separated as the oils rise to the top.

JEWEL BEETLES

Buprestidae

One of the world's most exquisitely beautiful edible insects, the vast family *Buprestidae* covers 15,000 species that are renowned across several continents for the iridescence of their elytra (wing cases), ranging over a huge spectrum of colours and patterns. In east Asia the beetles are bred solely for use as decoration for clothing and jewellery, but in Africa they are considered a nourishing and easy-to-access food source in many communities.

Not the brainiest of insects, they opt to fake death when shaken from their homes in trees, and are therefore easy pickings for insect harvesters. Once caught, their heads and extremities are removed and they are roasted. Larvae of many species of *Buprestidae* (such as the giant jewel beetle) are eaten in a similar way. A female beetle full of eggs is seen as a particularly lip-smacking delicacy in the Kalahari.

Taste: When roasted, their meaty insides taste like venison. Locally, the taste is said to be similar to eland (a type of antelope).

Country: Zimbabwe, South Africa, Botswana, Cameroon.

Habitat: A vast range of habitats from grassland to forests.

Dangers: They must be squeezed to remove the excrement, which has an unpleasant taste.

How to cook/prep: The wings must be removed along with the gut, then they are briefly roasted in ash and hot sand. At home, you could cook them over the white coals of a dying BBQ for a similar effect.

LAKE MIDGES

Chaoborus edulis

In central and eastern Africa vast numbers of midge flies are often seen swarming over lakes, emerging in time with the lunar cycle, and attracted by shoreside lights. They only live for a few hours, which they spend frantically reproducing and laying eggs. Although tiny, their sheer numbers create huge black clouds. Around Lake Nyassa (between Malawi, Tanzania and Mozambique) these swarms are known as *kunga* and are harvested with nets or oil-wetted pans and pressed into dense protein-, iron- and calcium-rich midge burgers known as *kunga* cakes. The cakes can be divided into burgers or dried for crumbling into stews. One of these cakes currently resides, lonely and uneaten, in London's Natural History Museum.

Taste: Musty and marshy, but with a strong savoury depth.

Country: Uganda, Tanzania and Malawi.

Habitat: They tend to congregate around lakes.

Dangers: None.

How to cook/prep: The cakes are dried and then boiled with tomatoes, onions, oil and nut paste.

KUNGA BURGERS
(MIDGE BURGERS
IN SCOTLAND)

Ingredients
Enough lake flies or midges to make a burger
Roughly ¼ onion per burger
½ garlic clove, crushed
Seasoning
Plain flour for dusting
Oil for frying

Method

- Mix your flies together with a splash of oil and stir until they are a pâté-like consistency.

- Grate the onion into the mix, add the garlic and seasoning to taste, and shape into 1cm-thick patties.

- Shape into burgers and dust with a little flour. Fry the burgers on a high heat in ample oil for about four or five minutes on each side. Check that they are cooked all the way through before serving in a soft bun with ketchup, a slice of tomato and a crisp leaf of lettuce.

EMPEROR MOTH CATERPILLARS (KANNI)

Cirina forda

A startlingly-spiky larva popular in African cuisine, this infant of the pallid emperor moth is one of the prettier edible caterpillars. It is traditionally harvested and hawked by women and young girls in the markets of middle and west Africa, who thwart the caterpillars' attempts to become butterflies right at the last minute as they are climbing down from the shea trees to the ground to begin metamorphosis. The caterpillars are highly nutritious and contain a high percentage of protein and vitamins.

Taste: Depends on how they're cooked, but they can taste like fresh hazelnuts when roasted.

Countries: Nigeria, Zambia, Zimbabwe and Democratic Republic of Congo.

Habitat: Sandy soft soil around their host plant.

Dangers: None known.

How to cook/prep: They are harvested through the rainy season from July to September, then soaked in boiling water and salted before roasting. In Nigeria they often feature in a rich vegetable soup.

BAGWORM MOTH PUPAE

Several species are edible, especially *Deborrea malgassa*

Bagworms are houseproud little creatures, building themselves little 'bags' in which to hide: extraordinary cases made from silk, leaves, twigs and sand. Although they can be considered pests due to the damage they cause to orange trees and wattle, several bagworms are considered edible in Central African Republic and Democratic Republic of Congo. In Madagascar, one particular species known locally as *fangalabola* is considered a delicacy. It's a native species of bagworm, and is encouraged to breed on wattle trees so that its pupae can be harvested. The bags they create are 35–55mm long, and they seem to prefer the *Acacia dealbata* tree.

Taste: Crunchy texture and juicy innards with an unsophisticated protein flavour similar to chicken.

Countries: Madagascar.

Habitat: Forests.

Dangers: None known.

How to cook/prep: Collect and wash pupae, then roast in the embers of a fire or the last hot coals of a BBQ.

MOPANE WORM

Gonimbrasia belina

A hugely important food in many parts of southern Africa, the mopane worm is actually a type of caterpillar waiting to become an emperor moth, and it gets its name from the mopane tree on which it's usually found. They provide valuable nutrition (including a higher protein content than beef) to millions across Zimbabwe, Botswana, Namibia, South Africa and beyond, and are variously considered to be a bushmeat or a delicacy depending on where in the continent you're standing. They are a economically important, particularly for harvesters in rural areas who can make money collecting and processing them. The worms are gutted, roasted (to remove the spines) and dried so that they can provide both stable protein and a source of income throughout the year. The ability to trade them as a dried commodity makes the harvest attractive enough to draw people from hundreds of kilometres away to the mopane woodlands; 9.5 billion caterpillars are thought to be harvested across southern Africa annually. The downside is that populations of the mopane caterpillar are under threat in some areas because of over-harvesting, and in Zimbabwe populations have at times been severely depleted.

Taste: Eaten dried they are almost tasteless, but protein-rich none-theless. Rehydrated and used in food they have a protein-rich beefiness and sometimes a slight mustiness.

Country: Found all over southern Africa from Botswana to the Democratic Republic of the Congo.

Habitat: The grubs live in trees and scrubland and are now harvested on a commercial scale.

Dangers: None known.

How to cook/prep: As they are available only at specific times of the year they are often preserved and are available sun-dried and eaten as a crisp-like snack. Alternatively, they can be smoked, which adds to the flavour, and sold in a can and eaten in a tomato and onion sauce with maize porridge. Fresh, they are squeezed out of their hard skin like toothpaste and their green guts are carefully removed.

CONGOLESE MOPANE WORM CURRY

Ingredients
50-100g dried mopane worms
2 onions, finely chopped
Splash of oil
1 tsp turmeric
3 red chillis
4 cloves garlic
1 tbsp finely chopped ginger
1 tin chopped tomatoes
200g okra

Method
* Soak the worms in water for at least four hours to rehydrate.

* Gently fry the onions in a little oil until translucent (around 10 minutes).

* Throw in the turmeric, then the sliced chillis, garlic and ginger and cook until fragrant (usually around one minute).

* Add the chopped tomatoes and okra and simmer for 20 minutes.

* Add the drained worms and cook until soft but still a bit crunchy.

* Serve with bugali (cornflour mash) or fufu (yam/plantain/cassava mash).

HISSING COCKROACH

Gromphadorhina portentosa

The poor, maligned cockroach seems to get a universally bad press everywhere other than Madagascar, where the arrival of these (actually very clean) insects is celebrated with the sharpening of cutlery. They are the only group of cockroaches that can hiss, forcibly emitting air from adapted breathing holes on the sides of their bodies. They use this quirk socially, either to attract mates or (in the case of the male) to intimidate rival cockroaches during epic battles with their horns and abdomens. Rather strangely, they've made cameos in a large number of films, from *Men in Black* to *Team America*, usually in a role more nefarious than delicious. But why? Well listen, I'm a pretty adventurous entomaniac who's unfazed by most creepy-crawlies but I have to admit to finding these little beasts terrifying. I don't know why, but when I pick them up and they curl their bodies and hiss, I turn to jelly. Better on my plate than in my hands.

Taste: Like chicken, but with extra crunch.

Country: Madagascar.

Habitat: Forest floors.

Dangers: Cockroaches give off a mild neurotoxin when raw that numbs the mouth and slows down chewing, but are harmless when properly cooked.

How to cook/prep: Wash, dry and roast.

PALM WEEVIL LARVAE

Rhynchophorus ferrugineus

This is the red palm weevil's larva, also known as the sago worm. It's a species of snout beetle larvae that causes devastation to palm trees (making it the arch-enemy of the palm oil industry). I first encountered them in a snack shack outside a train station in Cameroon, where the deliciously grumpy woman behind the grill poured a plastic carrier bag full of them into a hot, dry pan, and they cooked and hissed and wriggled for a while. When they wriggled no more, she skewered them and threw them on to a plate in front of me, along with a warm glass of sweet Guinness, as I tried to work out whether I was in culinary heaven or hell. The larvae are long: mostly around 5–6cm (and occasionally larger), and they delight in feeding on the soft fibres found inside palms. The female palm weevil can lay 300–500 eggs at a time, forcing them into the palm flesh with remarkable strength (and can even shove them into sugar cane, which is extraordinarily tough). Interestingly, the larvae are also fond of a banana.

Taste: Gutsy, squishy (due to their high fat content) and creamy, with a rich underlay of umami taste. When well salted they are almost bacon-like, with a similar heady savouriness.

Country: Hot countries worldwide. These larvae have spread as far as the Mediterranean and are eaten in many places, especially central Africa, Indonesia, and Papua New Guinea.

Habitat: Chop down your rotting palm tree (and occasionally banana, sugar cane, apple or squash) and hack out the crumbling innards to find these bugs after they have destroyed its flesh.

Dangers: None if well-cooked.

How to cook/prep: Wash in fresh water, then dry-fry or grill over charcoal.

NSENENE LONG-HORNED GRASSHOPPER

Ruspolia baileyi, and others in the family *Tettigoniidae*

A very popular snack in Uganda, *nsenene* have been eaten for centuries as a seasonal snack enjoyed twice a year during the rainy seasons. Traditionally they were harvested by the women and children, then exchanged with husbands for a new dress. These days long-horned grasshoppers (also called katydids or bush crickets) are a major source of income, with foragers attracting them with lightbulbs, nets and even their hands. They look oddly un-grasshopper-like and more shrimp-like when bought at market as they have had their wings and legs removed, and they are best enjoyed with a crisp Ugandan beer or sweet Nigerian Guinness. In Kenya the same grasshoppers are thrown directly on the fire in the hope that the smoke will scare away ghosts.

Taste: Similar to crispy chicken when fried.

Country: Uganda.

Habitat: Fields and grasslands, but fairly ubiquitous come the rainy season in Uganda where twice a year during May and November, it's peak grasshopper harvesting season.

Dangers: None if cooked thoroughly and de-legged – the legs are quite scratchy and can cause choking.

How to cook/prep: Legs and wings must first be removed and then they can be cooked in a variety of ways, from frying to roasting.

NDOKO

Strigocossus capensis (also referred to as *Xyleutes capensis*)

The castor bean borer *Strigocossus capensis* moth is a stem borer found across central and southern Africa, laying its eggs in cassia and castor bean bushes and several others. It's from the same family, *Cossidae*, as the witchetty grub and it's particularly interesting because it's both a pest and a delicacy. There have been suggestions that it could be semi-cultivated: cassia plantations that have experienced infestation problems could be redesignated as food production sites, sacrificing the trees for a better return of edible caterpillars. The caterpillars are relatively hairless and can take up to three years to mature and pupate.

Taste: When roasted they are rich and beefy.

Country: Although found across central and southern Africa, they are mostly eaten in Tanzania and DRC.

Habitat: Inside cassia trees and castor bean bushes.

Dangers: None known.

How to cook/prep: Clean, squeeze the guts out and roast.

ASIA

If you really want to earn your insect-eating stripes, you need to head to Asia, and specifically south-east Asia. It's the world's great entomophagy powerhouse – due not to the variety of insects eaten (which is barely half that of the Americas), but to trade. Insects are readily available in many markets (especially in north-eastern Thailand), making it easy to experiment, and there's also been an explosion in large-scale farming to complement rural foraging: there are now an estimated 20,000 cricket farms in Thailand alone, producing animal protein with a remarkably low ecological impact. In rural areas, families and friends team up after dusk to forage for (unfarmable) grasshoppers in the fields. They sell to local middlemen who ship the huge bags of live grasshoppers to town, earning the foragers some extra cash whilst at the same time tackling crop damage. But it's in south-east Asian street markets that unforgettable culinary adventures are to be found, and that's where I hope the guide you currently hold in your hands will be indispensable.

TOP 5 TIPS FOR BUYING INSECTS AT MARKETS

1. ***Eat 'em FRESH.*** The best insects are freshly cooked in front of you at busy stalls, with locals dropping in on mopeds, on foot and occasionally in chauffeur-driven cars to pick up a bag.

2. ***SEX.*** If you're told 'This is a terrifyingly powerful aphrodisiac and it'll definitely keep you at it all night', it's probably best to look at your partner and raise a cynical eyebrow. But when they've turned away, go ahead and buy a load anyway, just in case. But not if it's *Lytta vesicatoria* (Spanish fly). That stuff is dangerous.

3. ***WARNING.*** Don't eat a giant water bug whole. It will tear strips off your oesophagus, as it did mine. And take advice: if the stallholder advises you to pull the wings off first, do it.

4. ***PHOTOS.*** It's rude to take photos without asking first and then handing over ten baht.

5. ***TIME YOUR SUPPER.*** If you're buying insects at 8pm they've probably been cooked fresh and you'll have a blast. If you're eating them as a dare at 4am after a skinful of hooch, they will have been out in the warm for quite a while and you may experience gastrointestinal desolation the next morning.

LOCUSTS

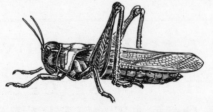

Many species of the family *Acrididae*

'So what's the difference between a locust and a grasshopper?' I hear you ask. Well, that's all down to behaviour. Whereas grasshoppers are relatively solitary, locusts can, under certain conditions (when they sense that the population density is high, causing crowding and pressures on food supplies), alter the serotonin production in their brains and become gregarious, changing their colour and body shape and forming dense migratory swarms. Locust swarms have plagued humanity for centuries, with one famous swarm of Rocky Mountain locusts in 1875 made up of an estimated 12.5 trillion insects and covering 198,000 square miles. But they are beautiful creatures and they make fine eating (the clue is in the name, deriving from the Latin *locusta*, which means both locust and lobster). They are sanctioned in the Bible and Torah as a decent foodstuff: Leviticus says 'Even these of them ye may eat: the locust after its kind, and the bald locust after its kind, and the cricket after its kind, and the grasshopper after its kind.' They make quite cute pets, even in cool countries where they don't traditionally thrive.

Taste: Nutty and very crunchy. Deliciously savoury – almost beefy – when freshly fried, although the legs can get stuck in your teeth.

Country: Found worldwide, and eaten with gusto in many Asian and African countries.

Habitat: Hot countries, across many types of vegetation, especially arable land.

Dangers: None known.

How to cook/prep: Deep-fry.

HONEY SPICED
LOCUST NIBBLES

NB this is a recipe for use with *fresh* locusts.

Ingredients
500ml vegetable oil for deep-frying
Handful of fresh locusts
2 tbsp honey
1 tbsp cayenne pepper
1 tsp cinnamon

Method
- Pour the oil into a deep, heavy-bottomed saucepan and heat until a small chunk of bread sizzles in it and turns golden-brown.

- Carefully drop the locusts into the oil and fry for 3–5 minutes until browned and crispy.

- Remove the locusts from the oil and allow to cool a little.

- Place the honey, cayenne pepper and cinnamon in a bowl and mix together.

- Toss the locusts in the honey mixture and serve warm.

HONEY BEES

Family *Apidae*

The grubs of many species of bee are eaten all over Thailand and in China some natural medicine practitioners use them in an attempt to reduce flatulence, counteract toxicity and kill worms. Honey bees are called *mang non won* in Thailand, where they are prized as food and of course as producers of honey, which can be as expensive as an imported bottle of whisky. They often taste smoky because of the method by which they are collected: a fire is lit directly under their hive to drive away the adults, while the pupae are smoked inside.

Taste: Depending on the cooking method the larvae can be slightly aromatic and sweet, tasting a little like cow's milk. They can also be bought canned (although, as with canned versus fresh olives, they will have an inferior taste).

Country: Honey bees are widely eaten in China and Thailand.

Habitat: Bee nests can be found in small trees and shrubs or high up on cliffs.

Dangers: None when cooked correctly (the gut should be removed from the larvae before cooking).

How to cook/prep: Adult bees are eaten raw – first the head is crushed and pulled off along with the wings, then the underside of the abdomen is eaten. Pupae are given slightly more attention and are cooked in coconut milk with onion, peppers and lemongrass. Alternatively they can be eaten directly from the comb with the honey.

GIANT WATER BUG

Belostomatidae

These vast freshwater bugs (of the order *Hemiptera*, or 'true bugs'), crop up across the world in streams and ponds and are extremely aggressive predatory carnivores, ambushing their prey with a vicious bite and injecting a saliva that liquefies their insides. The largest species in this family can grow to over 12cm, although most of those found freshly cooked in markets are *Letherocerus indicus* and are a bit smaller than a credit card – and once in the mouth they are almost as tough. I ate them in Thailand, where they had been caught at night using a bright light and scooped up in a net. Suffice to say, their tough exoskeletons are an acquired texture (which I never managed to acquire). Instead I landed a sore throat that lasted the entire fortnight I spent trying to make a documentary about the darn things. On the plus side, this species has a very modern approach to relationships, which we could all learn from: after mating, the male shows his appreciation of his paramour by letting her lay her eggs in beautiful patterns across his back (the females have a wondrous sense of symmetry). The female then says cheerio and promptly heads off to find another squeeze, leaving her partner to push the pram until they hatch; this makes it difficult for him to swim and impossible for him to mate. Go, girls!

Taste: The exoskeleton is pretty tough, but if you were being generous you could compare it to elderly biltong. Some people just pull the back wings off and discard them, digging into the gooey insides, which offer a strong (and not entirely unpleasant) musty, meaty flavour.

Country: Worldwide. Eaten with gusto in south-east Asia.

Habitat: Often found lurking in wait for their prey at the bottom of freshwater streams and ponds. They fly at night, so if you want to catch them during the breeding season use a blacklight (UV lamp) to lure them, and a good net to gather them. The main season in Thailand is June.

Dangers: In culinary terms they pose few dangers; as long as they are properly cooked, they should be safe to eat. But take care when foraging for them as they have *occasionally* been known to bite humans. Apparently it's excruciatingly painful.

How to cook/prep: Toss in a light batter of rice flour seasoned with a little salt and sugar. Drop them straight into a wok of very hot, fresh oil and fry until crispy. Then serve with a nice chilli sauce.

SILKWORM PUPAE

Larvae of *Bombyx mori*

Ubiquitous in the markets of south-east Asia and beyond, these pudgy, bloated caterpillars are an important and enormously popular food source and are generally farmed rather than foraged. They are the same species as that used for the production of silk, and sometimes households will raise them for both purposes, eating the pupae once the silk has been extracted from the cocoon (once the cocoon has been formed the caterpillar immediately sheds its caterpillar exoskeleton and reveals the pupa underneath). They are a major by-product of the silk industry and are used in numerous ways in food: boiled, fried, ground into a powder for flavouring other dishes such as curries; they are also available canned and are used as animal feed. They have an astonishing nutritional profile: 55% protein and 32% relatively healthy fats. In Chinese traditional medicine they have long been deployed to relieve flatulence.

Taste: They have sweet juicy flesh, a musty smell and an earthy taste. Their high levels of protein make for an intensely savoury flavour, which is why they are sometimes dried and ground into a powder and added to other foods in the way that we add glutamate-rich Parmesan to pasta dishes.

Country: Many countries where silk production is important, especially Vietnam, Korea, Thailand, Cambodia, China and Japan.

Habitat: Primarily farmed, and fed on leaves from the white mulberry bush.

Dangers: None known.

How to cook/prep: In Korea they are often simply steamed or boiled, but there are many ways – try steaming or stir-frying. Bake them first to dry them out, then stir-fry with ginger and garlic, fresh chilli and Chinese rice vinegar, and add crispy vegetables.

CATERPILLAR FUNGUS

Moth: *Hepialus humuli*
Fungus: *Ophiocordyceps sinensis*

One of the world's most bizarre insect-produced consumables, caterpillar fungus is actually the result of an unfortunate infection commonly suffered by ghost moth larvae by the *Ophiocordyceps sinensis* parasitic fungus. This fungus makes for a lucrative harvest; in Beijing it's highly sought after as a cure for every ailment from cancer to erectile dysfunction and, depending on supply and demand, it can be worth up to twice its weight in gold.

In Tibet this fungus is called *yartsa gunbu*, which means 'summer grass, winter worm' and refers to the fungus infecting (and killing) the larva before, in the spring, erupting grotesquely from its head as a brown stalk, leaving the exoskeleton intact. Over-harvesting of the hijacked larvae has led to a severely depleted population, threatening the multimillion-dollar *yartsa gunbu* industry. People have been killed in disputes over the caterpillar fungus and it was fought over by Nepalese Maoists and government forces during the Nepalese Civil War. All of which puts *Ophiocordyceps sinensis* into a box marked 'entomophagic curio' rather than 'viable food'.

Taste: Musty, mildly fishy-smelling.

Country: Found in the Himalayas, northern India, Tibet, parts of China.

Habitat: High-altitude plateaus.

Dangers: None known if properly cleaned and checked for other harmful fungi.

How to cook/prep: Traditionally soaked in water and then made into a tea. After drinking the tea, the leftover larvae and fungus are eaten.

SHELLAC

Excretion of the lac beetle *Kerria lacca*

If you ever need to stop small children gorging themselves on sweets, sit them down with a few jellybeans and tell them all about shellac. It's made by a scale insect from the superfamily *Coccidea* (which also includes the cochineal beetle; see the South America section), and the insects have developed an extraordinary ability to secrete lac resin pretty much constantly. They use this resin to build a hard casing around the branches of a tree, within which they can scuttle about, sucking sap and secreting more resin. They also secrete a wax and a dye.

The lac farmer, who has infested his trees for this specific purpose, cuts down the branch and then hacks off the brittle shellac and purifies it. Food companies then use it to help preserve sweets and add a lovely shiny surface to them. At this point it's often given the food additive name E904, so take a look at your shiny sweets and you might find that their glossiness is the result of beetle secretions. Shellac is best known for its use in cosmetics, French polishing and, in the old days, for making 78rpm records. It's also used on some pills for its ability to withstand the acidic environment of the stomach long enough to release the pill's contents further down the digestive tract.

Taste: None. It's just used for cosmetic and preservation purposes.

Country: India and Thailand.

Habitat: On the branches of the *Ziziphus mauritiana* tree, also known as the ber tree.

Dangers: None known.

How to cook/prep: Knock a chunk of shellac off the tree, then heat to liquefy and strain to purify. Leave to harden.

RED ANTS

Oecophylla smaragdina
Also known as weaver ants and green ants

These vicious little tree-dwelling beasts give a painful bite, but it's all worth it, because fresh (not canned) red ant salad is one of the best dishes I've ever tasted in my life. And in addition to the satisfaction of biting the little bleeders back, there's the sheer thrill of eating something so far removed from any definition of 'comfort food'. They are caught using a long pole with a net hanging below it, ready to catch the ants. The end of the pole is used to break into the nest, and then to shake it as the ants drop out. Although many ants and eggs get into the net, hundreds escape and jump or crawl down to start biting you. It's the larvae and pupae that are preferred (although personally I love the crunch and sourness of the adults). Kill them by dropping them in a bucket of water for a few seconds (and stir to stop them from making drift nets on which they can escape).

Taste: Naturally zesty from the acid in the adult ants, there's also a sweet creaminess from the larvae and pupae and a light crunchiness from the legs and exoskeletons.

Country: North-eastern Thailand, where they're a sought-after (and expensive) delicacy.

Habitat: These are found in a band crossing India, Thailand, Indonesia and northern Australia. Their nests hang in high trees and they are mainly hunted during the late summer season, when certain areas have dozens of heavy nests hanging 10–20m high in the trees, attached to the branches.

Dangers: The bites hurt a LOT, and the ants are tenacious. A few people are allergic to the venom and may require anaphylaxis treatment, although my experience was that the bites were non-venomous and after the initial pain, they left no bump, scar or itching.

How to cook/prep: Red ants are usually eaten raw in a salad – eggs, baby ants and adults all together. The salad is 95% ants and eggs, ant it's mixed with coriander, spring onions, sesame oil, rice vinegar and a little sesame oil.

BAMBOO WORMS

Larvae of the grass moth *Omphisa fuscidentalis*

Known as *rot duan* ('express train') in Thai, these aren't worms at all but the larvae of moths that infest bamboo. They are also a prized delicacy, commanding a much higher price than beef. After hatching, the larvae work communally to bore into the tough bamboo, and then before they get down to the busy work of laying down fat for their pupation, they bore a hole ready to escape from when they finally turn into moths in a couple of months' time. I tasted these during an illegal visit to the jungle villages of eastern Myanmar where the Karen ethnic group were in the midst of a vicious conflict with the army; the larvae were served to me with great pride.

Taste: In Thailand they are mostly deep-fried and served salty, like crisps with lots of extra protein, but the ones I had in Myanmar were simply fried in a dry frying pan and they had the most extraordinary taste – a lingering sweetness on my tongue, much like the inulin sugars that give Jerusalem artichokes a lingering taste.

Country: Thailand, Myanmar and Laos.

Habitat: Inside bamboo stems, mostly during the months of June and July.

Dangers: None known.

How to cook/prep: Dry-fry or deep-fry, then season with salt.

RHINOCEROS BEETLES

Oryctes rhinoceros, Xylotrupes gideon

Another delicacy from the rich insect-pickings of Thailand is the flamboyantly-horned rhinosceros beetle *oryctes rhinoceros* (known as *mwang kwang* in Laos). *Xylotrupes gideon* also deserves admiration for its impressive fighting ability – beetle fighting used to be a popular gambling sport but was banned because so much money was changing hands. They are considered a real treat by the Lahu people, who relish a roasted rhino beetle with chilli sauce. Larvae can even be bought online in canned form in Europe and they are a fantastic source of protein, containing double that of chicken and beef. These beetles are very strong and are capable of lifting up to 850 times their own weight.

Taste: A lovely earthiness similar to snails.

Country: Very common in Thailand and all over Asia.

Habitat: The larvae can be plucked from the rotting wood of the palm tree. The main Thai season is around September.

Dangers: None if cooked correctly (the gut needs to be removed from the larvae before cooking).

How to cook/prep: The beetles are usually roasted with their wings off but are occasionally fried, or even cooked inside a coconut shell. Larvae are wrapped in a banana leaf with herbs and spices, then barbecued or soaked in coconut oil before roasting.

BLACK ANTS

Polyrhyachis

The *Polyrhyachis* genus covers a vast number of species – nearly 700 – of wildly differing habits and habitats. They are 5–10mm long, but the ones most often eaten are definitely at the smaller end of the spectrum. They taste zesty, like many ants, and even those bought online, dried and canned, are pretty good. The taste is down to the formic acid that they spray using an extraordinary piece of anatomy, unique to ants, called an acidipore. It's a circular hole on their abdomen dedicated to the 'gaster' (the bulbous posterior), or stomach where the formic acid and other hydrocarbons are made. It's unclear whether the formic acid stings the ant in a post-vindaloo fashion when it's called upon to squirt its poison at a predator.

Taste: Lively and zesty, together with an exhilarating crunch.

Country: Found across Africa, Europe and Asia.

Habitat: As there are so many species in the genus, you're likely to find them anywhere from trees to water.

Dangers: None known.

How to cook/prep: Rinse, dry and roast.

DUNG BEETLES

Scarabaeinae

Despite the faecal association, dung beetles are exquisite creatures. They enrich the soil by recycling it, thereby providing an invaluable service to the environment, and are the only creatures other than humans known to orient themselves using the Milky Way. There are many species of dung beetle, including the famous 'rollers' that roll spherical balls of dung around to fill with their eggs. This rolling action is the easiest way for them to move and hide the balls quickly. On hatching, the larvae simply eat their way out. Yum.

They are considered such a treat that in parts of Thailand villagers reserve piles of dung containing the beetles by placing paper signs on them. Both the grubs and the adult dung beetles are eaten and are a rich source of protein. Dung beetles occupy a relatively prominent place in literature (among beetles at least), starring in *Aesop's Fables*, Kafka's *The Metamorphosis* and in a Hans Christian Andersen fairy tale (called, rather simply, *The Dung Beetle*).

Taste: As with many types of beetle they are reminiscent of shrimp, but with a slightly earthy note.

Country: Found on every continent except Antarctica.

Habitat: Nearpiles of manure. In Thailand the main season is around February/March.

Dangers: None recorded but they must be properly cleaned.

How to cook/prep: Soak the beetles in buckets of water overnight to ensure they lose any ingested dung. In Thailand they are then cooked in a little oil and salt, and in some areas of China they are baked then ground to a flour.

CENTIPEDE

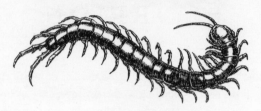

Scolopendridae

Another of our minibeasts that isn't actually an insect – this one is a myriapod (meaning 'many-legged'). Considering the voracious appetite across Asia for adventurous eating, it's surprising that the centipede isn't found on the menu more often. In China, I've only found them at Beijing's night markets, stuck on skewers after being deep-fried or grilled (but this does seem to be be a bit of a gimmick to attract tourists).

In a few other countries across the region, large examples of the species are kept submerged in alcohol, in a style similar to that of Meixan agave worms. The centipedes are meant to lend the spirit medicinal properties.

Taste: They are often cooked so thoroughly that they taste of little but hot oil and dried spaghetti. However, when cooked more delicately they can be quite bitter.

Country: Laos, Thailand, Cambodia and China.

Habitat: Under rocks.

Dangers: Some species of centipede can deliver a painful and potentially dangerous bite, so species identification is important before preparing them for dinner. Best to ask a local.

How to cook/prep: Deep-fry for a moreish crunchy texture! Make sure you season them well because their flavour can be quite bland.

SCORPION

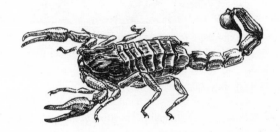

Family *Scorpionidae*

Another vicious, tantalising mouthful that isn't actually an insect but, possessing eight legs, a member of the arachnid class.

Scorpions are predatory, with big and powerful pedipalp pincers and a highly visible venomous stinger, usually carried high and proud, curved over their back and ready to kill you in your sleep. If you wanted to design an animal to elicit terror in humans, you'd be hard-pressed to do better than this. Actually, only a handful of scorpions have the venomous capability to kill a human, and they can also be very docile: I once held a large one in my hand, and was disappointed by its lack of interest in my delicious flesh (though it may have been put off by my copious sweating). Scorpions are a very successful order, found on all continents except Antarctica (they can even be found in the UK) and they have an evolutionary history going back 430 million years. They also have a bizarre ability to glow under UV light, and their glow gets stronger as they mature – with each exoskeleton that they shed (by 'moulting') they glow brighter.

Taste: Like centipedes, scorpions are on offer at Beijing's tacky but rather fun night market, where young men eat them to impress their dates. They are deep-fried and skewered on kebab sticks. Cooked this way they have the texture of Twiglets and taste of old oil. I'd avoid them and instead seek out more rural communities where scorpions are properly appreciated, and where, deep-fried they taste of pond-water mustiness and roast beef. When used as an ingredient in soups you really only sense the texture: slightly chewy.

Country: Mainly eaten in China, but found worldwide.

Habitat: Although we think of scorpions as inhabitants of hot countries, they can cope with a surprising range of temperatures from extreme heat to well below freezing. They are nocturnal creatures, so during the day you'll usually find them in holes or hidden under rocks or in little burrows.

Dangers: Although only a small proportion of scorpions are actually deadly to humans, some scorpion venom can be pretty nasty, so seek first aid if you get a bite. If you are served these raw, the poison sacs will have been removed, but best not to risk eating them raw at home! Happily, cooking renders the poison harmless.

How to cook/prep: Wash your live scorpions (carefully!), then stir-fry them in very hot oil (as with lobsters, you can stun them by popping them in the freezer first). Add ginger and garlic and crunchy vegetables, then pour in water, soy sauce, chillis, Chinese vinegars and rice wine before simmering until everything's tender.

HORNETS
AND WASPS

Vespidae

Not exactly the world's most cherished insects, wasps and locusts are generally considered nasty little things, spoiling picnics and buzzing around causing misery across the globe. The Shan of Myanmar (and many other cultures across Asia) have managed to leapfrog this loathing to appreciate the finer aspects of *Vespidae*; namely that they are delicious, especially in pupal form. The adult wasps are chased away by the deployment of large amounts of smoke.

The Japanese are really into wasp eating and serve larvae as *hachi-no-ko*, cooked simply in soy sauce and sugar, served with rice. Adult wasps are served in a sort of biscuit and there's even an Omachi Digger Wasp Lovers Club. Kashihara (in Honshu) hosts a whole festival devoted to wasp consumption with competitions to find the heaviest wasps' nest. Hirohito, an emperor of Japan, reputedly ate wasps after having surgery in 1987, choosing them over other more common dishes.

Taste: The pupae are slightly sweet with a velvety texture. In biscuits, adult wasps are said to be slightly raisin-like with a slightly bitter aftertaste.

Country: Found worldwide, enjoyed across south-east Asia.

Habitat: They nest in quiet spaces where they are won't be disturbed.

Dangers: The sting of the hornet can be very nasty – the Asian giant hornet has been known to kill up to 40 people a year in Japan alone.

How to cook/prep: Larvae should be cooked with soy and a little sugar, and adult wasps roasted (the sting should of course be removed). The Nordic Food Lab recommends a flower salad with marinated larvae, and both the pupae and the larvae are delicious with tempura.

BABY WASP NORI SUSHI ROLLS

Ingredients
300g sushi rice
Splash of sushi seasoning
Nori seaweed sheets
1 tbsp mayonnaise mixed with ½ tsp wasabi paste
1 cucumber cut into long thin strips
1 can of wasp larvae (available in Japanese shops)

Method
- Cook the sushi rice as per packet instructions, and finish with an extravagant splash of sushi seasoning (or make your own with 1 tsp salt and 1 tsp sugar dissolved in 2 tbsp rice vinegar). Stir it gently.

- Leave to cool in a wide tray while preparing the other ingredients.

- Lay out the nori on a sushi mat, shiny side down.

- Pat out the rice into a 1cm layer on top of the seaweed, leaving the 2cm edge furthest from you clear.

- Spread a thin layer of the mayonnaise over the rice and then lay your cucumber and wasp larvae down the middle of the rice.

- Fold over the rice into a roll and seal the seaweed with a little water like a stamp.

- Slice into sushi rolls of your desired thickness. Enjoy with wasabi, pickled ginger and soy sauce.

TOP 5 REASONS GIVEN FOR EATING INSECTS IN NORTH-EASTERN THAILAND

1. *Tasty.* 75%

2. *Snack.* 65%

3. *Use as ingredients in cooked meals.* 48%

4. *Traditional medicine.* 48%

5. *As food seasoning.* 32%

SOUTH
AMERICA

It's not surprising that entomophagy is deeply ingrained in South America because, let's face it, the Amazonian rainforest is teeming with little critters. The Americas as a whole top the global list of different varieties of insects eaten, home to 39% of all commonly eaten insect species (that's a whopping 679 of them). And the finest of all is, in my humble opinion, the Colombian fat-assed ant, which is not only fat of ass but fat in flavour, with an extraordinarily heady smoky bacon-ness. I've found these highly seasonal treats in markets as far away as Oaxaca, and they are now exported on a small scale across the world as a bushtucker trial.

What really stands out in South America is the preponderance of indigenous groups who have been observed eating insects by inquisitive anthropologists and natural historians over the years: the Tukanoans, Bari and Cariban are just a few examples. The Guayaki of Paraguay eat the larvae and pupae of eight different wasp species and the Yukpa of northern Colombia were found in 1973 to eat insects from seven different orders, 22 genera and endless species, preferring many to fresh meat. And consumption is growing: as deforestation pressures begin to affect the availability of larger game, the reliance on insects is expanding rather than contracting. Another in the long line of reasons why entomophagy is an excellent idea.

STRANGEST SEXUAL PRACTICES OF INSECTS

My experience of creepy-crawly eating has often had lewd overtones, especially in Central and Southern America. My first taste of Colombian fat-arsed ants was accompanied by lewd hoots of laughter from a group of flirty Mexican girls making some hand gestures whose meaning I blush to guess at. Palm weevils were invariably sold to me with a wink and tarantulas featured at the bottom of a jar of rice liquor as an aphrodisiac. Anything to add 50% to the price!

1. One stick insect species has been recorded paired for 136 hours in a technique known as 'cock-blocking'.

2. Water boatmen 'sing' really loudly by rubbing their penises against their abdomen.

3. Earwigs have an emergency backup penis.

4. Massive sperm: the tiny fruit fly *Drosophila bifurca* produces sperm that are more than 20 times the length of its body.

5. Some bees ejaculate with such force that the tip of the penis is ripped off and left inside the queen.

HONEY

Product of the *Apis* genus

Obviously this is an insect *product* rather than an edible insect, but the biochemistry of honey is so fascinating that its story simply must be told. Many types of bees and wasps make honey but the most familiar variety comes from the honey bee of the genus *Apis* (Argentina is the world's third largest producer) and this is how it's made:

The bee inserts its proboscis into the nectary of sugar-rich flowers and sucks up nectar. This nectar enters the first part of the stomach, called the honey stomach, which retains nectar but lets most other matter pass through. When the bee flies back to the hive it regurgitates the nectar and then, sharing it with other bees, eats it again. And again and again. This multiple regurgitation process continues for anything up to 30 minutes, while the nectar is attacked by the bees' digestive enzymes and gastric acids so that the sucrose in the nectar hydrolyses (breaks down by the addition of water) into a mixture of glucose and fructose. When the bees think that it's ready for storage they put it into cells, then flutter their wings, evaporating more water from the sugary goo so that yeast and bacteria can't spoil it.

Taste: Sweet and floral.

Country: Worldwide.

Dangers: Female worker bees can sting.

How to cook/prep: Pour copiously over hot buttered toast.

FAT-ARSED ANTS

Atta laevigata

One of the finest edible insects on the planet, these huge ants are a leafcutter species known as *hormigas culonas* (literally 'big-arsed ants' in Spanish) and revered in Colombia. And they are, indeed, fat of arse. Only the females are eaten and they are only collected for a few weeks every year, at the end of the rainy season around April. Harvesting them can be a painful affair as they have a vicious bite, provided by their large, strong mandibles. I have bought these freshly harvested in markets in southern Mexico, too, and unlike many insects they travel well and can be bought across the world, whether in cans or packs, as a treat or gimmick food. Real gastronauts should head to Barichara, a beautiful Spanish colonial town 300 kilometres north of the Colombian capital Bogotá, where fat-arsed ants are sold in shops and restaurants. Once caught, they are soaked in salty water and roasted, which imparts a wondrous flavour and excellent texture. They are regarded as an aphrodisiac by some locals.

Taste: Gutsy smoky flavour similar to smoky bacon crisps. They give a salty wallop of protein to the tongue and are nicely crunchy.

Country: Colombia, Venezuela and Paraguay.

Habitat: Forests and jungle – wherever there is a good supply of fresh vegetation.

Dangers: None if well-cooked.

How to cook/prep: Wash in salty water, then roast.

HONEY WASP

Brachygastra mellifica

This species of wasp, which is an important pollinator of avocadoes, is usually harvested across South America in the last quarter of the moon and eaten along with its honey. In Mexico the mixture of wasp and its honey is called *cuchii*. Unwise though it may sound, several kinds of wasp are eaten in South America: in Guyana wasps called *ocomo* are eaten as larvae and the Yukpa of Colombia are known to eat the larvae of a number of species of social wasp including *Polybia ignobilis* and *Polybia canadensis*. Nests are located during the day, then harvested at dusk when the wasps are calmer, and the nest is then kicked on to a fire to dislodge the adults. The larvae are quickly roasted on the fire and shaken out into the hand. Other wasps are strictly off the menu – the Yukpa believe that the *Eumeninae* mason or potter species cause blindness. Some tribes in the Amazon Basin are reported to insert wasps into breastplates with holes on the inside, allowing them access to the body. These are worn and used in purification ceremonies as an ordeal by stinging.

Taste: The larvae are distinctively sweet and mildly eggy.

Country: Found across South America and sothern North America.

Habitat: They build their nests in trees and shrubs.

Dangers: They sting.

How to cook/prep: Roast in a fire or BBQ, the young are eaten raw.

DOBSONFLIES

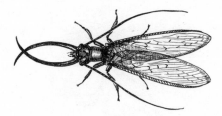

Family *Corydalidae*

The aquatic larvae of the dobsonfly isn't, let's face it, the prettiest of edible insects, resembling as it does a muddy cross between a lobster and a woodlouse. Found in several countries across the world, they are often used by anglers in trout fishing. However the Yukpa, a tribe that ranks fairly highly on South America's list of insect scoffers, consider the dobsonfly and its larvae a useful snack. When caught as adults the wings, head and legs are removed before the body is roasted. *Helgrammites*, the name given to the larvae stage of the dobsonfly, are also eaten in parts of China and Thailand.

Taste: Mildly fishy.

Country: Colombia, Peru.

Habitat: The dobsonfly lives in shallow rocky streambeds, feeding on other smaller larvae.

Dangers: They can bite and are best handled with care.

How to cook/prep: If cooking the adults, remove the wings, heads and legs before roasting.

COCHINEAL

Dactylopius coccus
From the *Hemiptera* order of 'true bugs'

These little scale insects are the entomophagist's cheeky joke on anyone who wouldn't dream of eating bugs – because it's almost impossible to avoid them. They're used extensively by food companies as a pink/purple/red food colouring – especially in gummy sweets and pork products – mainly because this means the food company can write the words 'No Artificial Colouring' on the label. And for this reason, the cochineal industry is booming. The bugs contain an intense red colour called carmine, also known as E120 or sometimes simply 'cochineal'. Most come from South America, although several countries have attempted to farm them, with mixed results (Australia's attempt ended in the death of the bugs, while the cactuses they'd been imported on eventually overran 259,000 square kilometres in eastern Australia). On the cactus leaf they look like a mouldy mess covered in dust, and once harvested and dried, they look like small pieces of dark greyish gravel. Only the female bug is harvested – the males are weedy and don't eat, mainly because they don't have mouths. They live for a week: just long enough to grow wings, mate and die.

Taste: Raw, they are a little bitter, but once processed into carmines and used sparingly in food, they have little or no discernible flavour.

Country: South America – mainly Peru (85% of global production), Ecuador, Chile, Bolivia.

Habitat: Cactus plants of the genus *Opuntia*.

Dangers: As a food additive, there have been very occasional reports of it causing anaphylactic shock, but it is tightly regulated. If you have been advised to avoid E120, avoid cochineal.

How to cook/prep: Using a mortar and pestle, grind a little pinch of 15-20 bugs into a fine powder and drop them into cake icing or yoghurt to give it a rich pinky-red colour. If you add it to a pint of water, you'll turn it bright red, but as the carmines are unprocessed and unstable, they will slowly oxidise and change colour to black.

LEMON ANTS

Myrmelachista schumanni

These ants are famous for two things: firstly their strange symbiotic relationship with the *Duroia hirsuta* tree. The ants nest in the hollow stems of these trees, and have such a close relationship that they explore the forest, poisoning all the other trees and plants by injecting formic acid poison into the base of their leaves. This creates a desolate area called a 'devil's garden' of the single tree species to the exclusion of all others.

Their second claim to fame relates to that same formic acid – it offers the adventurous explorer a delightful zestiness to lighten the sweaty task of navigating the rainforest. Admittedly they are very small ants, so they aren't a huge source of calories, but they are delicious nonetheless.

Taste: A lemon- or lime-like zestiness as well as a little crunch from the legs and exoskeleton.

Country: Across South America.

Habitat: Rainforest. They are easy to find by the clearings they create around the *Duroia hirsuta* tree.

Dangers: None known.

How to cook/prep: Gather a few in your hand and munch them raw.

DRAGONFLY

Order *Odonta*
Suborder *Anisoptera*

These elegant predatory insects have large double wingsets that give them an extraordinary flying ability, combining a zippy agility with cruising speeds of 4.5m/second and maximum recorded speeds of 10–15m/second. They are similar to damselflies, but are better pilots and their wings are held perpendicular to the body when at rest, whereas the damselfly folds its wings parallel to its body. Most striking are the dragonfly's compound eyes, with up to 24,000 ommatidia (little lens-like clusters packed with photoreceptors) arranged spherically, giving them nearly 360-degree vision. Their vision is hugely important to them; an estimated 80% of their brains is dedicated to processing visual information. They even have special brush-like tools on their legs for cleaning their eyes. The dragonfly spends the vast majority of its life as a nymph and usually only days in its beautiful adult form.

Taste: Their spindly shape offers a high surface-area-to-volume ratio, which means that when they're fried, thanks to the Maillard reaction you get a lot of savoury flavours. So they are meaty and crunchy, and occasionally musty (like many insects). When the insides are still soft, the experience can be a *little* like eating soft-shelled crab. But only a little.

Country: Worldwide. As their common wetland habitats are being destroyed or degraded in some places, they may become threatened, so keep these to a rare treat.

Habitat: Wetlands, near fresh water and ponds, although they are strong fliers and will travel far for food. Can be caught using a stick coated in sticky sap.

Dangers: None known.

How to cook/prep: Wash, dry, then toss in flour and fry in very hot oil (coconut oil if you have some). Season well, then scatter coriander on top and serve with small bowls of soy sauce. They are sometimes kebabed on wooden sticks or twigs.

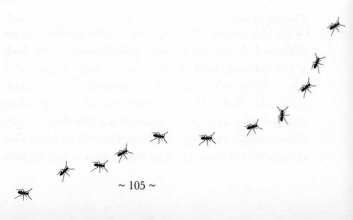

WHITE JUNE BUG

Platycoelia lutescens

The white June bug is known as *catzos blancos* or *catzos con tostado* in Ecuador, where it's appreciated as part of the culinary tradition of the Quito region. Between October and November catzos foragers will rise at 5am to catch the beetles as they emerge to mate, plucking them from the ground before taking them straight to market to be sold (or home to be eaten). They are traditionally prepared by removing the wings – the bodies are then deep-fried in pork fat and eaten with tostadas, a corn-based toasted snack.

They are in season for around a month, so they can command a high price at market. The elytra or wing cases of the beetles were used for jewellery by Inca women, and their presence used to announce the start of the planting season; if the beetles were in short supply it was thought to be a bad omen for the year's harvest.

Taste: The experience is mainly textural – very fatty, crunchy and nutty.

Country: Ecuador.

Habitat: They live underground, usually, in meadows, before emerging as adults with the first rains.

Dangers: None if prepared properly.

How to cook/prep: Soak the beetles in flour for a day, then drain and place in a bowl of water. Remove the wings and legs before frying in fat – traditionally pork fat, but oil or butter will do admirably.

CATZOS BLANCOS

Ingredients
As many June bugs as you can collect
150g fine white flour
300g lard for frying
Corn on the cob or toasted corn

Method

* Firstly, place your live beetles in a large bowl and sprinkle with flour. Leave overnight and in the morning remove the wings and legs.

* Soak in cold, salted water for a few hours and then remove and leave to dry.

* Heat the lard until it sizzles.

* Fry the beetles in batches until golden and crisp and serve fresh with barbecued corn on the cob or toasted corn.

TARANTULA

There are many species of food-worthy tarantula across the world, especially those in the *Theraphosidae* family. These are hairy arachnids rather than insects, but they are so fascinating they had to be included! They make great eating despite their scary reputation, and many are not dangerous to humans. They hunt using surprise ambushes and generally eat insects and other spiders, although the largest specimens can kill mice, lizards and smaller snakes. They are found throughout South America, the USA, Asia, Australia and southern Europe. Their burrows don't run in straight lines, so unless you have expert guidance, catching tarantulas is both terrifying and unwise. You have to dig into the burrow, checking with your hand to see which way the hole leads, before digging in that direction and checking again. Eventually you will come to the tarantula, which can be caught by pressing down on its back with a twig to stop it escaping. If you can stop yourself from shaking with feat for long enough, then pick it up with a firm squeeze on either side of the 'waist', ensuring that its fangs, which hang on the underside, are out of reach. Kill by squeezing hard on the back or dropping into a bucket of water. When pickled in rice liquor, they are said to have a powerful aphrodisiac effect, although this is probably more due to the alcohol and the exciting frisson of fear than anything the spider has to offer.

Taste: Rich sweet crablike meat – when seared, they develop grilled seafood flavours similar to langoustine. Abdomen creamy and soft, legs similar to soft-shelled crab.

Habitat: Found in many different environments including trees, forests and dry rice fields, often lurking inside small holes which are disconcertingly similar in size to an open human mouth.

Dangers: These are venomous; a bite can cause a very nasty swelling and, if you're susceptible to it, anaphylactic shock, so best to leave the catching to the experts. The poison is neutralised by cooking.

How to cook/prep: Wash, dry, salt, then grill over charcoal and eat whole.

GRILLED TARANTULA

Ingredients
1 fresh tarantula spider
Salt
Bowl of rice, prepared according to packet instructions
Chilli flakes
Fresh lime, quartered

Method
- Wash and dry your tarantula.

- Toss in salt.

- Grill over a barbecue or open fire for 4–6 minutes, turning frequently until crispy.

- Place the tarantula on a bowl of rice, scatter with chilli flakes, squeeze lime over the top and serve.

NORTH
AMERICA

Ten years ago, the most common reaction to the mention of entomophagy in the USA was nervous laughter. Today, however, there's a new breed of eco-conscious foodheads and adventurous eaters who are willing to taste rather than laugh; companies are experimenting with high-protein insect powder to fortify foods, especially protein bars; and purpose-built edible insect farms are beginning to crop up in the news. Of course, North America has form in this area, with historical reports of native Americans eating many insects. Research in the Great Basin has indicated that insects used to be an important food resource, especially shore flies, crickets, grasshoppers, caterpillars and ants. And there's exciting stuff happening either side of the US. To the south, Mexico has a rich, ancient culture of insect-eating, producing vast quantities of delicious chappulines (one of my all-time favourites); and to the north, Canadian company C-fu Foods is looking to the future with some sumptuous-looking 'sustainable pasta sauces': Cricket Bolognese and Mealworm Bolognese.

TOP 5 STRANGELY ALLOWABLE INSECT CONTAMINATION IN USA

I love the USFDA (US Food and Drug Administration). With a straight face and a formal tone, they have tackled what few countries are brave to countenance: the inevitability of insects and insect fragments getting mixed in with agricultural goods. And they've put numbers on them! We are truly blessed. You can use this handy list to tick off those you've already eaten:

☐ *1. Canned sweetcorn.* 12mm (in length) of corn ear worms or corn borers per 11kg sweetcorn.

☐ *2. Canned citrus fruit juice.* Five or more fly eggs per 250ml (or one or more maggots per 250ml).

☐ *3. Frozen broccoli.* Average of 60+ aphids/thrips/mites per 100g.

☐ *4. Hops.* 2,500 aphids per 10g hops.

☐ *5. Ground thyme.* 925 or more insect fragments per 10g.

MAGUEY WORMS

Aegiale hesperiaris and *Hypopta agavis*

You may have come across the maguey worm bobbing around the bottom of a bottle of mescal (they are also known as agave worms) and wondered if it's just a gimmick. Well, in Mexico it's a little bit more than that. These aren't actually worms, as it happens, and they come in two main types: red ones (caterpillars of the *Hypopta agavis* moth) and white ones (caterpillars of the giant skipper butterfly *Aegiale hesperiaris*). They both infest huge agave plants that are grown to make into spirits, much to the chagrin of farmers. Their parents lay eggs at the heart of the leaves, and when they emerge, they feed on the sweet flesh at the base of the plant. There's also a third worm called the agave snout weevil that's sometimes popped into bottles of hooch; all are a real pest for farmers, who can lose up to a third of their harvest to them. Consuming them as food is a small but significant act of revenge, and the worms are sometimes added to bottles of mescal for their flavour.

Taste: In markets around Oaxaca they are sold pre-cooked and skewered on long strings, but you can sometimes find a pinch of them served ground into a powder and served alongside a cold Mezcal beer. The idea is to dip a slice of lime into the powder and then suck it for a salty/sour umami mouthful alongside your drink. On their own they are usually fried or stewed with chilli, and they offer a whole world of umami, salty, meaty flavours.

Country: Mexico – mainly central and southern but can be found at markets in most cities.

Habitat: At the base of agave plants. Chop down the plant with care (they have pretty vicious spikes), and you'll invariably find some maguey worms within.

Dangers: None known.

How to cook/prep: If you find them fresh, wash them and fry them with chilli and salt. Excellent added to an egg and cactus patty – as an ingredient they act like little chunks of bacon.

AHUAHUTLE

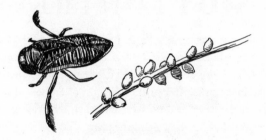

Also known as *axayacatl*
Eggs of several species of aquatic *Hempitera*

Famed as a Mexican version of caviar (as are *escamoles*), these expensive little eggs have a long and noble history as a food enjoyed by Montezuma, and also by the Spanish conquistadores. Writing in 1557, the historian Sahagún described how special runners were employed to rush the fresh eggs in from Texcoco (25 kilometres north-east of Mexico City) to the emperor's table in time for breakfast. The eggs were known as *aguaucle*, meaning 'seeds of the water'. They are laid on vegetation in lakes or stagnant water by various aquatic insects of the *Hemiptera* order of 'true bugs'. They are tiny little eggs, usually 0.5–1mm in diameter – the size of large sand grains – and are often sold dried in markets. They are semi-cultivated by collectors who anchor floating bunches of twigs as egg-laying sites.

Taste: Crunchy and slightly marshy. At a stretch, you could say they were like caviar, but it's one heck of a stretch!

Country: Mexico.

Habitat: Lakes and among rushes, as well as floating on the water.

Dangers: None known.

How to cook/prep: Mix with egg and chopped cactus and make into little burgers for frying.

COTTONTREE WORM

Stenodontes damicornis
Family *Cerambycidae*

Residing, as the name suggests, in cotton trees, this is the plump grub stage of the longhorn beetle *Stenodontes damicornis*. Known locally as *maucoco* or *cusi*, it was widely eaten in Jamaica in the past, in soups and pottages as well as roasted over fire, and is ripe for culinary resurrection. Various recipes exist, some dating back to the eighteenth century; the general consensus is that the creatures taste best rolled in breadcrumbs and scattered with a few spices. They are large (8cm long), and during the era of slavery, when they were considered a delicacy, some plantation owners would give one person sole responsibility for harvesting the worms from trees.

Taste: Rich, like bone marrow.

Country: Jamaica.

Habitat: They live in plum and cotton trees, burrowing through the wood.

Dangers: None if cleaned properly.

How to cook/prep: Rolled in nutmeg, salt and breadcrumbs then skewered and roasted.

CICADA

Order *Hemiptera*
Superfamily *Cicadoidea*

Surprisingly ugly for an insect synonymous with the lazy days of summer, cicadas have bulbous eyes set wide apart, large, clumsy and fragile-looking wings, a pudding-bellied abdomen and stumpy antennae and legs. Yet what a glorious racket they create. Unlike crickets and grasshoppers, which make their song by rubbing together comb-like serrations on their wings together, cicadas contract and relax internal muscles that vibrate membranes in their abdomen called tymbals. The extraordinary volume of the cicada is thought to result from the enlarged chambers in their body that make the sound resonate.

Common across Northe America, they are already a highly regarded food source in Malawi, where they are collected using reeds or grasses covered in gluey substances, which stick to the cicadas' wings. North Americans should be posed to do the same – both the cicada nymph and the adult can be eaten.

Taste: As with many similar insects, these are usually deep-fried, lending them the flavour of the oil that they have been cooked in, plus a light nuttiness and the root taste of fried protein – similar to chicken.

Country: Found worldwide, mostly in tropical regions, including 170 species north of Mexico, and one (best left uneaten due to its extreme rarity) in the UK.

Habitat: Many different types of habitat – trees, tropical wetlands, deserts, rural and urban areas. The hotter the country, the more populous they tend to be.

Dangers: None known.

How to cook/prep: Wash and deep-fry.

CICADA FLORENTINES

Ingredients
50g butter plus extra for greasing
50g brown sugar
50g golden syrup
50g plain flour
6 cicadas, blanched, wings and legs removed, sliced in half lengthways
100g chocolate (plain or milk)
30g pecans, chopped up
50g candied lemon

Method

- Grease two non-stick baking sheets using a dab of butter.

- Heat butter, sugar and syrup in a pan and heat until sugar has dissolved and butter melted.

- Add the plain flour and stir thoroughly, then add all other ingredients (except chocolate).

- Spoon out a teaspoon of mixture per Florentine on to baking sheets lined with greaseproof paper, making sure there is a lot of space for them to spread during cooking.

- Cook for 8–10 minutes at 180°C (350°F/ Gas Mark 4) until golden-brown, then take out and leave to cool and harden. When hard enough to move, place them on a wire tray to cool further.

- Melt the chocolate in a bain-marie (a heatproof bowl placed over a saucepan of boiling water), then paint it over the top of the Florentines.

PANDORA MOTH

Coloradia Pandora

The larvae of the Pandora moth are eaten by the Paiute Native Americans of California, who call them *piagi*. They spend their first year living high in the branches of trees eating pine needles, and gatherers of the delicacy can tell where the caterpillars are congregating because of the large number of telltale droppings found at the base of the tree.

After harvesting, the Paiutes place the larvae in trenches before covering them in hot sand and roasting them until the hairs and legs fall off. After this they are left to dry and can be stored in salt for a year or more. When ready to be eaten the dried worms are rehydrated in water then boiled and eaten as they are, and the cooking liquid is used as a base for soup.

Taste: Not a huge amount of aroma, but the savoury protein taste can be quite powerful.

Country: California.

Habitat: The caterpillars spend their first year in branches of the Jeffrey tree before coming to the forest floor to pupate – it is at this point that they are harvested.

Dangers: None if cleaned and cooked properly.

How to cook/prep: Roasted in hot sand for thirty minutes or so.

STINK BUGS

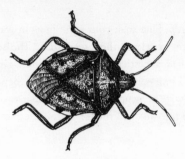

Halyomorpha halys

Regularly eaten in Mexico, China, south-east Asia and southern Africa, the stink bug was accidentally introduced to the USA (first spotted there in 1998) and the brown marmorated stink bug has become a serious agricultural pest, especially in orchards. So it's time to get our own back by chowing down on them. These little fellas are just 17mm long and their smell-producing glands are on their undersides. The smell they create as a defence mechanism is oddly herby and spicy – much like coriander (with which it shares some volatile flavour compounds), which may not sound like a bad thing, but if one makes its smell in your house it can linger for hours.

Taste: Crispy and crunchy and, depending on how they're cooked, can have a slightly fruity taste. They are eaten raw in Africa and Asia, but this can give you a numb mouth. If the 'stink' juices are not removed (see below), they will have a bitter taste.

Country: Found in many countries including the USA, Japan, Taiwan and China, and eaten especially in Indonesia.

Habitat: Found as a pest among apples, beans, mulberries, figs and many ornamental plants. Harvesting is generally easier on colder mornings as the bugs are (like most insects) more immobile when the weather is colder.

Dangers: The stink bugs' defensive odour can cause allergic reactions in some people, leading to rhinitis, conjunctivitis and occasionally dermatitis.

How to cook/prep: First soak your stink bugs in warm water – this encourages them to release their secretions. The soaking water is sometimes used as a pesticide against termites. Don't use boiling water as this will immediately kill the bugs, but they will retain their bitter juices. Roast, or wrap in foil (or strong leaves) and put the package straight into an open fire for 15 minutes.

ESCAMOLES

Larvae and pupae of various ant species including
Liometopum apiculatum and *Liometopum occidentale*

Several foods are nicknamed 'Mexican caviar', but *escamoles* are probably most deserving of the term because they are similarly rare, expensive and delicious. You can find them on sale in good markets, especially in Mexico City, tightly wrapped in long cylindrical plastic bags in salty water. They are the larvae and pupae of several ants and they are surprisingly large – about the size of a baked bean. Depending on the species, they are harvested from either agave plants (similarly to maguey worms) or underground nests and have become popular as part of a resurgent interest in traditional Mexican cuisine. They are also found – but not eaten – across the south-western states of the US, so there's a new market of inquisitive carnivores just waiting to be enlightened.

Taste: Creamy and sweet, when fresh they burst with a soft pop in the mouth. When fried, they have a soft egg or cheese texture.

Country: Eaten in Mexico but found also across south-western USA.

Habitat: The ants tend to make nests in rotting logs, agave plants and underground. Be careful – they are aggressive!

Dangers: None known.

How to cook/prep: Wash, then fry or poach them. Eat with guacamole or thinly sliced cactus leaf, or fry with eggs and eat on tacos.

GRASSHOPPERS

Order *Orthoptera*, suborder *Caelifera*

Grasshoppers are powerful jumping insects with large hind legs that look like spindly versions of a chicken wing. They fry extremely well and although they are eaten mainly in Africa and south-east Asia, they have also been a feast food for Ohlone Native Americans, and as they are plentiful pests in California, I hope to inspire the good citizens of the USA to transform pest into protein and take them to their hearts. Or stomachs. In Thailand they are found at roadside stalls, and customers will pay a pretty price as long as they are cooked fresh and the oil they are cooked in is not old.

They're easy to catch when you strap a large light to your head and deploy a fast snatching motion. Beware: the lamp on your head will attract every flying beast under the moon to wallop you in the face. Grasshoppers will often jump to escape, but as they seem to have limited intelligence, they tend to make a big leap and then get confused about where to jump next, allowing you a few milliseconds to swoop.

Taste: Crunchy to the tooth and (when well-prepared and fried in fresh oil) with a smell similar to roasted beef.

Country: Found worldwide. Eaten in many countries, especially China, Thailand, Cambodia, Mexico and historically in the USA.

Habitat: Anywhere there is vegetation, especially open countryside.

Dangers: None known.

How to cook/prep: Deep-fry on their own and serve with soy sauce as a snack, or roast and then add to a stir-fry.

CRICKETS

Order *Orthoptera*
Family *Gryllidae*

With a passing similarity to grasshoppers, but generally smaller and with a much reduced ability to jump, you may think that crickets are of less importance. But you'd be very, very wrong. Crickets are part of a huge food revolution as they are easily farmed and their FCR (Food Conversion Ratio) of 1.7 (the amount of food they eat compared to the amount of protein they produce) is much more efficient than beef, which has an FCR of 8 to 13.

There are many companies using not just whole crickets but also the high-protein flour made from them, which is added to pastas and protein bars. There has been a burgeoning cricket industry in Thailand for several years, where there are now an estimated 20,000 farms, and this is spreading to North America, with several farms beginning to produce for human consumption.

Thai farms are pretty basic: open-sided barn roofs with the crickets living in large wooden boxes full of egg boxes for them to hide in. Their land footprint, water usage and feed input is tiny in comparison to the amount of edible protein they produce. The farmers have an intriguing way of stopping the crickets from escaping: a single strip of shiny brown packing tape around the top edge of their box. They climb as high as this, then slip off.

The Ute Native Americans in Utah kindly fed hungry white settlers their 'prairie cakes' during harsh winters, which were enjoyed until the settlers learned that one of the ingredients was bush crickets. Then they refused to eat any more.

Taste: Nutty when eaten dried – like hazelnut or walnuts, to be specific. When deep-fried along with pandan leaves they make for a strong, oily, meaty hunk of protein, as though you had deep-fried a slice of beef.

Country: Found worldwide, and farmed in many countries, including the USA, Canada, Europe and across south-east Asia.

Habitat: Fields, among many crops including rice, corn and cereal.

Dangers: None known.

How to cook/prep: Wash, then deep-fry. Also excellent as the protein ingredient in salads and stir-fries.

CORNBREAD CRICKET MUFFINS

Ingredients
100g polenta
100g cricket flour
100g self-raising flour
3 tsp baking powder
1 tsp salt
4 tbsp sugar
450ml buttermilk
2 eggs
Knob of butter

Method
➤ Mix dry ingredients in one bowl, wet in another and combine.

- Grease a muffin tray and pour in the mixture, making sure you leave some room at the top for them to rise.

- Bake at 180°C (350°F/Gas Mark 4) for 15 minutes or until a skewer comes out clean.

CHAPULINES

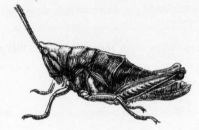

Genus *Sphenarium*

These grasshoppers are a hugely popular Mexican delicacy, and feature alongside smoked duck guts, maguey worms, marsh flies and fly eggs as part of a traditional food revival in Mexico City and beyond. They also happen to be among my top five entomophagic treats and are particularly prized around Oaxaca, where various different grades of them are sold piled high in mounds on wicker baskets. They colour a deep red when cooked (much like lobsters), and are most often eaten on their own as a snack food rather than as an ingredient, although they are sometimes used in tacos. After washing, they are roasted on clay with chilli, lime juice and salt (although garlic and lemon varieties make excellent eating, too). They are often sold after the large rear jumping legs have been pulled off (they have little barbs that can be a choking hazard, catching in the back of your throat). The most expensive grades are whole pieces with abdomen and head intact, and the cheaper grades are often made up of leg pieces or offcuts. Chapulines are one of the handful of insects that are good to eat dry and preserved. They have appeared on the menu in my house for many years, and in a forward-thinking UK Mexican restaurant chain called Wahaca.

Taste: A fabulous mouthwatering sour-saltiness combined with a tang of chilli and an excellent protein-rich roundedness. These are a truly fantastic food, and ripe for marketing to barfly braves across the world.

Country: Mexico, especially around Oaxaca.

Habitat: Ubiquitous in cornfields and across the countryside.

Dangers: None known.

How to cook/prep: Wash them thoroughly, then toss in chilli, salt and garlic. Squeeze lime over them, then place in an unvarnished clay cooking plate, and roast until crispy.

OCEANIA/ JAPAN/ PACIFIC

Just when you thought the famous witchetty grub must be Australia's most strange and wonderful food, along comes the honeypot ant: a lozenge in insect form. And then you learn about lerp, the honeycrust coating left behind by aphids. It becomes clear that Aboriginal Australians have been enjoying the wilder side of entomophagy for hundreds of years.

On the other side of the Pacific, Japan is a whole different kettle of *zaza-mushi*. It must have one of the most adventurous cuisines in the world (only in Tokyo have I ever been served cod sperm, horse sashimi, micro squid, deadly fugu and still-twitching fish – all on the same day). But in terms of insects, while anthropologists have offered much historical evidence of historical Japanese entomophagy, it's mainly bee and wasp larvae and braised caddis-fly larvae that are available nowadays (although fried and soy-seasoned rice grasshoppers, *Oxya japonica*, also known as *inago*, are available; but mainly as a luxury item). Don't let the small scale of Japanese insect-eating put you off, though: when the Japanese cook something, they cook it exquisitely. And after all, wasp larvae and rice was a favourite dish of Emperor Hirohito.

TOP 5 INSECTS CONTAINING THE MOST PROTEIN

Witchetty grubs look, to most westerners, like a cruel culinary joke. The sort of thing Roald Dahl would have invented if they weren't actually real. But the protein content of them, like so many insects, is phenomenal, making them a genuine nutritional marvel. Bizarre they may be, but insects also provide immense dietary benefits. How many of the below protein-rich species have you sampled?

❑ *1. Hymenoptera.* 13–77% (ants, bees and wasps).

❑ *2. Hemiptera.* 45–57% (true bugs).

❑ *3. Lepidoptera.* 14–68% (butterflies, moths including silkworms).

❑ *4. Coleoptera.* 23–66% (beetles).

❑ *5. Odonata.* 46–65% (dragonflies).

BOGONG MOTHS

Agrotis infusa

Dusty-looking, grey, fairly nondescript, heavily moth-like – on first impressions, the bogong moth does not scream 'epicure's delight'. Indeed, most moth-eating around the world focuses on the larvae rather than the adult iteration of this insect, but in the past these moths featured heavily in the diet of native Australians.

They can be eaten raw; you simply rip off the slightly fluffy wings, pop them in your mouth and enjoy their high levels of both protein and delicious fat. The larvae are known as cutworms because of the clean bites they take out of crops; it's worth noting that at this stage in their life cycle they are vulnerable to absorbing pesticides.

The adult moths undertake a vast migration, riding spring winds from Queensland through the Great Dividing Range to the Australian Alps to avoid the intense summer heat. There they hibernate in caves in large numbers – up to 17,000 per metre, clinging to the cold cave walls. When they emerge in autumn the same moths return to the breeding grounds, and next spring their offspring will repeat the cycle, despite never having made the journey before, a feat entomologists are still trying to understand. They were historically of great importance to certain tribes around the mountains, who would harvest them in vast numbers from the caves and hold inter-tribal meetings and feasts.

Taste: Buttery and walnutty. Close your eyes and forget about the moth in your mouth and you can just about claim a similarity to popcorn.

Country: Australia.

Habitat: During winter they live on the plains around Queensland, but migrate to high altitude areas around Victoria when temperatures start to rise.

Dangers: Because of widely used pesticides and herbicides in some areas, there is a risk that large-scale consumption could put you at risk of arsenic poisoning. Check local practices before you eat too many.

How to cook/prep: Remove the wings, then either eat raw or roast. Historically they were harvested by scraping them off the walls of the caves with a stick, or by stunning them with smoke and collecting them on kangaroo hides as they fell to the floor. When roasted they were mashed together to make 'moth meat'.

MOTH PÂTÉ

Ingredients
A large quantity of adult bogong moths
150g cream cheese
100g crème fraiche
Lemon juice
Pepper

Method

* Heat your oven to 200°C/Gas Mark 6.

* Place the moths in a roasting tray and roast until crispy but not burnt. Allow to cool and then pull off (and discard) the wings and heads.

* Blend them in a food processor and add cream cheese along with the crème fraiche. Blend again until you have a smooth mixture. Season with lemon juice and salt and pepper.

* Use your moth pâté as a spread on toast.

KING CHRISTMAS BEETLE LARVAE

Anoplognathus viridiaeneus

The larvae of this gorgeous, golden-brown beetle from the scarab family are a popular snack for Aboriginal Australians. The beetle emerges in the summer, towards the end of December (hence the 'Christmas' part of their name). They have tiny little barbs on their legs, and the grubs tend to dine on the roots of grass, making them the foe of Antipodean gardeners, who hate the resulting brown patches on their lovely lawns. Luckily for them, but sadly for everyone else, the species is in serious decline in response to the development of Sydney as a major city on their turf, so perhaps these are best kept as a rare festive treat. The *anoplognathus* subspecies are quite difficult to identify unless you count the individual hairs on their bums – a source of unending hilarity for entomologists.

Taste: Musty and very mildly eggy.

Country: Australia.

Habitat: Rotten wood for the larvae; the adults feast on eucalyptus leaves.

Dangers: None recorded.

How to cook/prep: Can be sautéed or roasted over hot coals.

LERP
(HONEYDEW)

Austrochardia acacia and others

The word 'lerp' comes from the Australian Aboriginal *larp*, signifying the crusty coating formed by psyllid insects from the *Hemiptera* order that is collected by humans, birds and mammals for its delicious sugary hit. Hundreds of different psyllid species' larvae produce lerp on eucalyptus trees in Australia. The odd-looking crystallised sugary sap is used by some of the larvae as a protective cover and is often left behind as a by-product of their leaf-eating. It dries quickly in the sun, leaving a sticky, conical sugary pile – the lemon sherbet of its day. It is thought that lerp was given the thumbs-up in the Bible and Qu'ran as 'manna' – a dew-like treat. In North America the Indians of the Great Basin seasonally harvested honeydew; they would cut down reeds near rivers, then dry out the sticky sap to make it brittle and easy to handle, after which they'd shake it out on to hides. Once the honeydew had been dislodged it was rolled into balls and stored in baskets.

Taste: A subtle, starchy and fragrant sugary hit.

Country: Australia, North America, Africa and Japan.

Habitat: Lerp-producing aphids live on a number of plants, but seem to be very happy on eucalyptus trees. Sometimes whole trees were cut down to harvest the delicious substance.

Dangers: None known.

How to cook/prep: Used as sugar. In Victoria, Australia, lerp was traditionally diluted to make a sugary drink.

WITCHETTY GRUB

Several moth larvae, mostly those of the
cossid moth *Endoxyla leucomochla*

This is the Boo Radley of the entomophagy world. Its name (sometimes spelt 'witjuti'), refers to the *Acacia kempeana* bush on whose roots it feeds. Scary and vast as they are (growing up to ten centimetres long) witchetty grubs make excellent eating and are renowned for their ambrosial taste. They are an important bush-tucker food for Aboriginal Australians for good reason: they are packed with protein. They also belong to the small group of insects that are often eaten raw, whereas most insects are cooked (for reasons of both food hygiene and gastronomy). Despite popular TV programmes showing the eating of live insects as a challenge, this rarely happens in major entomophagic cultures, where they know that the application of heat makes for marvellous transformations to protein-rich foods as well as dealing with potential pathogens. Witchetty grubs are much tastier when baked, but munch them raw if that's what floats your boat. They are a hard-won food – not every bush will be infested with them, and they must be dug out using much effort in an environment that is often very hot and dry.

Taste: When raw, the witchetty grub feels fatty, wet and soft on the tongue, with an almond tang. When cooked in a fire, however, extraordinary chemistry kicks in to develop wondrous flavours: the taste is like scrambled eggs crossed with chicken, and with a nutty twist.

Country: Australia.

Habitat: They live deep within the roots of the witchetty (or *witjuti*) bush, and must be dug out with a long thin shovel.

Dangers: None known.

How to cook/prep: Eat raw if you fancy, or simply toss in the fire for a few minutes, then rescue them, scrape the charring off, and eat.

WITCHETTY GRUB KEBABS

Ingredients
10 witchetty grubs
1 red onion (cut into eighths)
1 aubergine cut into chunks
1 lemon

Method

- Skewer your grubs with the red onion and the aubergine and squeeze lemon juice over.

- Cook over a hot barbecue or under a hot grill until the bugs are crisp on the outside, like sausages.

- Squeeze on more lemon and season.

HONEYBAG

Hive of stingless bees from the tribe *Meliponini*

This traditional Aboriginal Australian food source is actually the hive (or 'honeybag') of the stingless native bee. Their habitats are declining due to human development, so it's probably best to view this entry as a fascinating diversion, but not as an invitation to eat! These tropical and subtropical bees do, in fact, have stingers but they are very small and can't be used by the bee to defend itself or its hive. Instead they can bite, and also secrete a nasty substance from their mandibles that can cause blisters; en masse they will physically defend their colonies. Although their hives produce a relatively small amount of honey (about one kilo per year as opposed to the commercial honeybee's 75 kilos per year), they are resurgent among ecologically minded suburban gardeners attracted by the lack of sting. Aboriginal Australians are thought to have tracked the bees' hives by trapping a bee and sticking a visible leaf to it so that they could trace it as it flew back to its hive.

Taste: Sweet, sour, fruity and with a viscosity thinner than commercially bought honey.

Country: Australia.

Habitat: Open countryside and trees.

Dangers: None known.

HONEYPOT ANTS

Melophorus bagoti and species belonging to
genera *Camponotus* and *Myrmecocystus*

'Repletes' are special worker ants whose sole purpose is to act as living honey tanks, storing nectar gathered by their peers in their distended abdomens. They haven't landed the plum role in the nest (if there is such a thing): they are unable to move, and spend their lives deep underground hanging upside down in specially built chambers while being fed flower-nectar and the sugary excretions of sap-eating scale insects and plant lice. When the distended ant's nectar is needed, the worker ants will stroke its antennae, encouraging it to vomit some of its sugary juice. The ants are the size of an M & M, which is handy.

Taste: Deeply sweet honey-like juice.

Country: A classic Aboriginal food in Australia, although they are found in many other countries in North and South America and Africa.

Habitat: Underground nests, mainly in arid environments.

Dangers: None known.

How to cook/prep: Wash the ants and bite the raw abdomen off.

STICK INSECTS

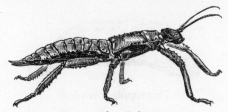

Eurycantha Calcarata

Not the most widely eaten insect but fascinating nonetheless, various the *Eurycantha Calcarata* species are eaten in Oceania. It's a Papua New Guinean heavily armoured, chunky stick insect species that feeds on the leaves of the forest such as ficus, bramble and guava. The males have an enlarged femur on each hind leg and large curved spines. They use these for defence by raising their abdomen in an alarming posture, then clamping those spines down on the potential threat (this really hurts as they are immensely strong). They also have exocrine glands behind their head that can emit a very strong and rather unpleasant odour if threatened. The Papua New Guineans are known to have twisted off these back legs where the spine is and use them as fishing hooks. I like to think of this practice as a two-for-one meal deal. The droppings of a certain type of stick insect, *Eurycnema versifasciata*, are made into a medicinal tea by the Malaysian Chinese and used to treat a number of ailments from asthma to aching muscles.

Taste: The eating experience is almost entirely textural, although if cooked well, the exoskeleton can give up a delightful roasted-prawn-shell smell and the flesh provides a subtle leafiness.

Country: Australia, Papua New Guinea, Malaysia.

Habitat: Palm and many other tree leaves.

Dangers: None recorded.

How to cook/prep: Best lightly roasted or deep-fried.

HUHU GRUB

Prionoplus reticularis

The huhu grub is the larva of a type of longhorn beetle and used to be a popular food among the Maori of New Zealand. The grubs spend two or three years pottering about in rotten wood, biding their time before they emerge in midsummer as lovely glossy beetles (the largest in New Zealand at 1.77 inches). From this moment on they no longer eat and concentrate instead on reproductive fun for the last two weeks of their lives. The Maori considered them to be most delicious just before the metamorphosis stage. When they reach their beetle stage they have a penchant for flying around at night and are considered quite clumsy, often crashing into windows and houses after being attracted by the lights. They are also known as 'haircutters' thanks to the many sharp hooks on their exoskeletons that make them hard to disentangle if they fly into your hair.

They are patently not the prettiest of insects, resembling a 7cm-long chubby maggot, but (like many grubs) they are packed with nutrients and fat.

Taste: Gooey inside with a simple, umami-rich chicken taste that can have a woody, peanut-butter tang.

Country: New Zealand.

Habitat: Lowland forests. They like to infest rotten tree trunks.

Dangers: None recorded.

How to cook/prep: The Maori used to eat them raw, but they are less challenging and slightly more palatable when sautéed.

MAORI HUHU AND PIKOPIKO SALAD

Ingredients

Ten huhu bugs
1 lemon
1 bunch pikopiko (foraged New Zealand fern sprouts)
100g chopped streaky bacon
100g wild mushrooms
1 bunch kokihi (New Zealand spinach)

Method

- Roast your bugs over hot coals until cooked through and crisp on the outside. Season with lemon juice and allow to cool slightly.

- Blanch your pikopiko as you would asparagus – leave it with a certain amount of bite.

- Fry the bacon until crispy, then add the mushrooms to the fat and wilt the kokihi in the same pan. Add your pikopiko and sauté until gently wilted.

- Serve warm with your huhu grubs.

ZAZA-MUSHI

Order *Trichoptera:* the aquatic larvae of caddis-flies. Many
Trichoptera species fall under the name *zaza-mushi*, especially
Stenopsyche griseipennis and *Parastenopsyche sauteri.*

The surprisingly large larvae of the caddis-fly, *zaza-mushi* can be eaten
in specialist restaurants in Japan, and are also sold canned. Their name
is a compound of the word for insects (*mushi*) and the onomatopoeic
zaza, associated with flowing rivers, and it doesn't refer to one single
species but rather any larvae that are catchable and toothsome. Not,
it must be said, the most attractive of insects (although if you say that
to an entomologist they will moan about pandas getting all the press
while the vast majority of biomass is ignored).

Taste: These tend to be cooked in sugar and soy sauce, so they taste of
… sugar and soy sauce, but with an undeniable savoury protein fullness.

Country: Japan, though they should be forageable wherever caddis-
flies are found in numbers.

Habitat: They live in gravel under rocks in flowing fresh water.
Locate your rock, then position your net downstream of it, and lift
said rock. The larvae should flow into your net.

Dangers: None known, but that really depends on the cleanliness of
the stream in which they were caught.

How to cook/prep: Stew them in soy sauce and sugar.

BARDI GRUB

Trictena atripalpis

These vast grubs are sometimes used as fishing bait, but such a waste of food would have doubtless horrified the Aboriginal communities who used to eat them with gusto. They are sometimes included in the catch-all 'witchetty grub' group, although this particular species feeds on different vegetation (eucalyptus or *Casaurina pauper* rather than *Acacia kempeana*). The adult incarnation of the bardi grub is known as the rain moth because it often emerges from the ground in the rainy autumn – and when they are aloft they are so big they can be mistaken for small birds or bats (female moths can have a wingspan of 16cm). To complicate matters further the term 'bardi grub' can also refer to the longhorn beetle larva *Barbistus cibarius*. They can be tempted from their lair by gently tapping on the ground near the opening to their burrow – this tricks them into thinking the rains have started, so they joyfully squelch their way to the surface, and Bob's your bardi grub.

Taste: Notes of warm cream and roast pork.

Country: Australia.

Habitat: Around the base of gum trees.

Dangers: None.

How to cook/prep: They are dug out of the ground with a large stick before being roasted briefly over a fire or coal BBQ. Sometimes the bugs can be quite deep underground, in which instance they can be retrieved with a hooked piece of wire.

Acknowledgements

Happy though I am to take all the credit for this book, I must grudgingly admit to the tiniest bit of help from dozens of brilliant entomologists, anthropologists, climate-change scientists, naturalists, statisticians, cooks and food writers whose work, both current and historical, I consulted, tickled and plundered. Special mention must go the UN Food and Agriculture Organisation for its publications and sheer enthusiasm, and also to the late Gene DeFoliart (whose extraordinary online bibliography is something of a gateway drug into entomophagy).

Particularly sumptuous acknowledgements are due to several people: the wonderful Hugh Woodward, whose efforts are reflected not just in the depth of information herein, but in some very fine turns of phrase, and for keeping me sane when I should, by rights, have gone stark raving locust. My entomologist friend Sally-Ann Spence kept the book in check and on track, and let me fiddle with Darwin's specimens at the Pitt-Rivers in Oxford. A huge thank-you to the fantastic Jessica Barnfield for suggesting this book and for editing it so well *despite* being a vegetarian. And a big thank you to Candela Riveros for her wonderful illustrations.

Many people are to blame for leading me on the path to entomophagic enlightenment, especially Daisy and Poppy (for the day they licked their fingers, dipped them into a jar of bug eggs and pronounced them 'delicious'), Georgia Glynn Smith (who, let's be honest, struggles to love insects), Kari Lia, Nik Porter, Nipaporn "Jam" Potong, Mark Collins, Will Daws, Karen O'Connor, Richard Klein, Clare Paterson, Cassian Harrison, Janice Hadlow, Jan Croxson, Borra Garson, the crazy tarantula boys of Cambodia, Brodie Thompson and Eliza Hazlewood.

Thanks to my beloved BBC – and the great British public for funding them – for sharing so many of my fascinations and obsessions.

And finally, thanks to all the ants, bugs, locusts, grubs, worms, spiders, gastropods and myriapods I've met on the way to writing this book. Sorry for eating you. But let's face it, if I didn't, something else would.

Notes from my culinary adventure

....

....

....

....

....

....

....

....

....

....

....

....

....

....

....

....

Notes from my culinary adventure

....

....

....

....

....

....

....

....

....

....

....

....

....

....

....

....

Notes from my culinary adventure

....

....

....

....

....

....

....

....

....

....

....

....

....

....

....